Praise for
Dad and I

"This engaging memoir spans the early years of Singapore's history with many vivid details about the socio-cultural life then. Shalini has captured many tender and loving moments between father and daughter, despite a restrained relationship. Her experiences during her growing up years and later as a working mother will resonate with many readers. In this way, this is not just the journey of one Malayalee family but is truly a Singaporean journey and story, one that all of us can identify with."

>Dr. Cheah Yin Mee
>Principal Consultant at Learning Ventures, Mindfulness teacher

"Shalini and Damodaran had me spellbound for a few hours. I laughed at the adventures of 'little Shalini' and her father's customers. She had me in tears, too, at poignant moments. *Dad and I* will take you to familiar places within you."

>Dr. Anitha Devi Pillai
>Teacher Educator, National Institute of Education, Singapore

"It's one of those books that I couldn't put down once I started reading it. Shalini definitely has a gift with words, and right from the start I felt transported into her father's life. As a silent witness, I learned about his courage to follow his dreams, the love for his family, his way of facing adversity, his strength, values, and, of course, life in Singapore at a time when I wasn't yet born. *Dad and I* is a beautiful invitation to seek out a more profound reconnection with parents, and others, for that matter, before it's too late. Rather than taking everyone in our life for granted, there is so much more to discover about each other when we genuinely want to know more about who they are, their dreams, concerns, values and joys. There are so many gems to be discovered in this book. Many times I sat there, parts touched within myself that were hidden before; often I paused to reflect and find inspiration. Thank you, Shalini, for sharing this journey with the world."

Antoinette Biehlmeier
Founder of TheraSmart, Owner of InnerDynamics Map, and Co-Founder of TimeWaver SEA

Dad and I

by Shalini Damodaran

© Copyright 2020 Shalini Damodaran

ISBN 978-1-64663-010-3

All rights reserved. No part of this publication may be reproduced, stored in a retrieval system, or transmitted in any form or by any means—electronic, mechanical, photocopy, recording, or any other—except for brief quotations in printed reviews, without the prior written permission of the author.

Published by

◀ köehlerbooks™

3705 Shore Drive
Virginia Beach, VA 23455
800–435–4811
www.koehlerbooks.com

DAD AND I

SHALINI DAMODARAN

VIRGINIA BEACH
CAPE CHARLES

*For Nishanker, Sandhya, Preshin and Nikhil
in memory of loving moments with muthacha*...*

* Grandfather, in Malayalam

Table of Contents

Author's Note 1

Chapter 1
MY FIRST HUG 7

Chapter 2
WHO WAS MY DAD? 13

Chapter 3
YOU CANNOT RUSH THE DYING NOR THE LIVING 21

Chapter 4
THE MARRIAGE 28

Chapter 5
THE RELEASE 37

Chapter 6
MOURNING. GRIEVING. REFLECTING. 45

Chapter 7
KAMPONG BAHRU DAYS IN THE '60S AND '70S 50

Chapter 8
THE MODEST ENTREPRENEUR 59

Chapter 9
THE SANCTUARY 68

Chapter 10
OPENNESS. DIVERSITY. INCLUSIVITY. PEACE. 74

Chapter 11
WHERE ARE OUR ROOTS? 82

Chapter 12
UNDERSTANDING DAD..93

Chapter 13
OUT OF THE SHADOW INTO THE LIGHT..100

Chapter 14
REFASHIONING THE BLUEPRINT... 115

Chapter 15
NOT KNOWING 132

Chapter 16
LET STILLNESS LIGHT YOUR WAY...137

Chapter 17
DISCOVERING THE UNLIVED LIFE THROUGH ART..................................147

Chapter 18
WRITING IN THE DARK—MEDITATIVE WRITING 152

Chapter 19
DEAR MUTHACHA..160

Chapter 20 167

Chapter 21 172

ACKNOWLEDGMENTS..179

Special Thanks..181

Author's Note

A MEMOIR IS IN many ways fictional, written from memory and stories related from remembrances. Memories as we know are selective, as are stories, open to embellishment over time. We remember what we want to: often we remember only the moments that have made us pop with emotion. We simply don't remember, or we ignore, a large part of our lives that goes by without ballyhoo. Sometimes, unknown to us, we treasure only memories that make for an exciting retelling. Those stories are rousing, provoking or thrilling. . . they stir the audience.

This memoir about my dad, and my relationship with him, is a story that was waiting to be birthed. Though it went into a long labour of love, it did eventually come out of the shadows to celebrate who my father was, and what he stood for. This endeavour was made possible only because of the several casual to formal conversations I have had with my mum about my dad's childhood and his early adult life. The formal discussions took place more recently once my intent to write my book became clearer to me. I would sit with my mum, with an agenda, to verify or clarify a story that I had heard. Otherwise, we would just natter. There were many stories that I would have heard a hundred times over, as she had the tendency to repeat those deemed to be of value, having put them through a little filter. I realized that she, too, was a storyteller reveling in a tale to delight the audience.

There were some stories, however, that I heard only once, and only after some prodding or querying. These were the gems, buried in the folds of my mother's memory because she may have thought them banal or uninteresting. Or they could have been moments that had simply slipped into chinks of her mind, comfortably wedged, for years, and forgotten. These treasures had to be gently excavated, and presented to the public eye with just enough polishing lest they lose their authentic lustre.

Deep listening is indeed an art and a skill. It requires inner quiet, contemplation and waiting. You can't speed up conversations nor recollections of moments. My mum would want to relate her stories in a willy-nilly, leisurely manner, wanting to relive and savour every moment and bring them back to life. But my mind would often drift in and out: looking at what went before, looking at what came after, and unkindly, at times, I would skip the here-and-now. Often, in the spaces between "what you hear and what you do not," there is an inclination to fill in the blanks with your own story. So, aware of my tendency to wander and waft, I would retell some of the stories back to her. It led to some hilarious conversations. My mum would go, "That's not how it happened." I would give her an incredulous look and mutter, "You sure that's not what you said? Remember, you had said that it was the tailoring guru who said…?" "No, I didn't. It was *acha*'s uncle!" My mum would then be delighted to retell the story all over again. She would be very sure that it was I who had lapsed.

As a writer, I've also had to actively resist the overwhelming desire to embellish or rewrite the stories of my dad that I heard over the years. It would surely make for a scintillating story if the hero makes a million dollars from naught, drives a swanky car and lives in a mansion facing the ocean with his secret mistress and two French Bulldogs. To fight off the urge to feed my own insecurities was as challenging as my need to give in to what I perceived as appealing to popular sentiment. On all counts, the integrity of the writer is inherently at stake, however hard one tries to avoid or resist the pitfalls.

This passage of time has been very special to me. Retracing and walking in my father's shoes has made me realise some truths about myself, and grasp how much of my father I have in me and how much I have fallen short. The more I wrote, the more I discovered and the more nuanced my understanding of my own beliefs, values and perceptions. It opened the floodgates to my past. A stream would have been easier to contain, but managing a torrent of emotions, episodes and experiences required support from family, friends and a professional writing coach. To all of whom I am deeply grateful.

Part 1

A Sentient Soul

What is the soul?
Wherefore does it live?
Does it have eyes that see,
Ears that hear,
A nose to suss out
What is or what is not?
To roam, or stay and languish at will?
Does it have a heart,
Feel pain and joy
And a mind that knows
Its body burdens not?

Chapter 1
MY FIRST HUG

IT WAS MY FIRST hug. Decades late, you might say, as I tried awkwardly to put my arms around my father to comfort him. He lay stiffly on the white sterile sheet of a single bed in Ward A of Tan Tock Seng General Hospital, breathing and feeding through tubes of oxygen and fluids. The doctors declared that he was unconscious. In medical terms, it meant that he was partly or completely unaware of external stimuli, but every now and then he would give out a loud, guttural heart-wrenching wail, which the doctors assured us was an involuntary reflex. How was I to be convinced? Every twitch, however insignificant, spoke to me. I felt he was desperately trying to reach out to us. Knowing my father, he was probably fighting to live, even if it was for another day. He was always tough, and it shattered me to see this strong silent man in agony. All my attempts to comfort him and say, "Acha[1], I love you" seemed to fall off the walls of Ward A. *It's too late*, I thought to myself.

I was struck at that moment by the chasm that lay between me and my dad. I just didn't quite know how to express my affection for him. Growing up, we never hugged. We never kissed. We never said "I love you" or expressed how deeply we appreciated each other. It was comfortable sometimes to let the day go by with not a single word passing between us. A nod here, a smile there seemed enough. And that's the way life passed us by, unsuspecting. My dad was eighty and I was forty-eight, a mother of two children, when my dad suffered a hemorrhagic stroke that rendered him unconscious.

---

1 *Father, in Malayalam*

In the ward, as I kept vigil, I kept wondering about the silence that befell me and my dad, the silence that I had grown accustomed to. Shaking his arm that fell to his side, I muttered, "Acha, can you hear me? Blink if you do, or move your fingers." I needed the assurance that he was aware of my presence. I needed him to know that I had not abandoned him, that he was not alone and that the entire family was there for him. But he lay stiff and unresponsive, breathing with his eyes half-open as if in a trance. His facial muscles had sagged after the stroke and he looked weak and undefended.

A couple of weeks before the stroke, on 24 December 2003, I was with my family, younger brother and his son at the Singapore Cricket Club, celebrating my daughter's birthday. It was the eve of Christmas, and we were in the midst of raucous revelers and gaily clad children making merry with party poppers, festive blowouts and mini hand clappers at the Club's annual Christmas Eve celebration, when I received a phone call from my mum that my father had chest pains. Though I couldn't remember a time when he had complained of any ailment, we thought nothing of it because my dad was up and about when we had left home for the Club. But to appease my mum, my husband and I left the party immediately. We were further convinced, on arrival at home, that it was minor after seeing dad walk down two flights of stairs unassisted, with my mum trailing behind him, to meet us at the car. His posture was as upright as always. He carried his usual sunny smile, and his words were audible and clear. He told us calmly, without wanting to alarm us, that his chest was painful. I don't think he suspected it was anything serious, though he did look somewhat shaken.

In his mind, he had always carried an image of himself as the young handsome man he had been some sixty years before. He kept himself trim and fit. He ate moderately, and gave up drinking even the occasional beer ten years earlier. He prided himself on being healthy and not being on any long-term medication. Amusing as it was, he referred to everyone his age or even half his age as "that old man." We were quite confident that this eighty-year-old "young man" was probably having muscle spasms, and we would soon be rejoining the rest of the family at the Singapore Cricket Club for my daughter's cake cutting.

We headed for Raffles Medical Hospital which was ten minutes away. Preliminary investigations revealed my dad had suffered a massive heart attack that had caused considerable damage to his heart muscles. The doctors were surprised that he had not collapsed. We listened to the doctor in disbelief. My dad, who listened with his gaze fixed on the doctor, was still smiling though I could see the creases of concern appear at his temples. He was in denial. We were, too. *This can't be happening.* The reality dawned on him when the doctor explained to him that he had to be admitted right away to the Intensive Care Unit of the hospital for further investigation. My dad, who had never been hospitalized before, looked defeated all of a sudden. His face now revealed age lines that all this time had been smoothed by an indomitable spirit.

The sudden shift from our happy celebration of life to what seemed like the possibility of death was surreal. My younger brother immediately left the Christmas Eve party with the children to join my husband, mum and me at the intensive care unit of Raffles Medical Hospital. I could see in my brother's eyes the same sense of disbelief, and a hope to be jolted from a bad dream. My son, who was twelve, burst into tears when he saw his granddad hooked up to heart monitors and defibrillators. Dad found his reaction surprising. He was touched. Smiling, he related the incident to my mum, perhaps feeling reassured that he was indeed loved. My daughter and nephew were both fifteen. Their response was muted, fearful as we all were of death and the loss of a loved one. They surrounded my dad in silence unable to fathom this day, a birthday celebration, that had unfolded so unexpectedly before them.

The doctors recommended an open-heart surgery, but they weren't sure if my father would survive such a procedure. After some deliberation among the family, we decided against it. I felt a strange heaviness in my chest constricting my air passage. I couldn't breathe. Most of the time you feel that life goes on forever. You see your loved ones every day, but do you really? My mind was strangely associating the heart attack to anger, regret and pain. His. *Was he angry about something? Did he have regrets*? I had no idea. That day at Raffles Medical Hospital, I entertained the thought that my dad's time was drawing to a close, and that I was not going to be able to turn the clock back. There simply was not enough time. I felt a sudden urgent need to do everything to make amends. I began arranging for my family and close friends to see him. It was almost as if I was preparing for a funeral, and I didn't want my dad to depart without saying his goodbyes. Surprised by my call, many of our relatives and friends who were fond of dad visited him at Raffles Medical Hospital. It felt like a small uplifting party of sorts in the ward. I think it was the first time in a long time that he felt the warmth, affection and the undivided attention of many whom he had known for a long time. The single ward filled up in no time with laughter and well wishes. I could see dad's face glow. It was a moment of awakening for me. I listened as never before. I began to notice the little things we often ignored in our daily attempt to accomplish all the various tasks that we deem to be of the utmost importance in our to-do lists. Time slowed down for me. It began to reveal many things to me about my dad. *He may have been lonely and he may have yearned for something more while he lived with us. Conversations and company, perhaps,* I thought to myself!

A week after his heart attack, he was discharged from Raffles Medical Hospital with a cocktail of prescription drugs in what looked like a grocery bag. Though he forced a smile, he looked decidedly impatient to get out of the ward. His farewells to the nurses with their usual pleasantries were perfunctory. Barefoot, he bounced from the ward to the car not betraying any hints of a failed heart, nor his impatience with a daughter who had forgotten to bring his sandals. How could I not have remembered something so important to him? His reminders to me seemed to have fallen on deaf ears. Nevertheless, he was soon his good old self, energised perhaps by the attention from friends and family.

He was relieved to be home. But for a man who rarely took any medication all his life, the prescription drugs that he had to contend with from day-to-day proved to be a burden. Still, apart from his daily struggle of having to imbibe capsules and tablets in different sizes and psychedelic colours, everything appeared normal until that fateful morning when my mother tried waking him up in vain. The last time she saw my dad conscious had been at 2.30 in the morning when she got out of bed to get a drink. My dad had done the same. She said that their eyes had met in the kitchen when he gave her a sad, forlorn look as if to bid goodbye to his loyal companion of fifty years.

He must have suffered a massive stroke in the wee hours of that morning. My mum had been alone at home with our helper that weekday when she tried desperately to wake him up for his morning breakfast of Milo and toast. My husband and I were at work and my children at school. My dad had always been an early riser, but today my mum found him unresponsive and unrecognisable. Something had changed. Assuming the worst but unable to utter what she really thought of the situation, she called my younger brother. "Mone[2], Acha is not waking up! Come now…"

My brother was surprised by the calmness in her voice. He expected her to be hysterical. But for him, too, time stood still. He called for the ambulance. How was this day going to end? It seemed like an ordinary day interrupted by a morning call. On arrival, my brother recalled being relieved to find my dad's heart still beating, though dad seemed to have lost all his senses. That morning, my brother sat beside dad in the ambulance to Tan Tock Seng Hospital,

---

2 *Term of endearment for 'son' in Malayalam*

speaking to him all the way hoping to shake him out of a state that he did not want to comprehend. He said it was one of the most harrowing experiences he'd ever had. The traffic that morning was unusually daunting; no one would give way to a screaming ambulance. Father and son were caught in peak hour traffic with busy people rushing to get to work, oblivious of two souls in distress.

Acha seemed to have left us that fateful morning. When I arrived at the hospital shortly afterward, he had no semblance of sentience, though the heart monitor registered a beating heart. If not for his heart-wrenching guttural wail that echoed through the Neuroscience ward, he seemed to have lost all his faculties.

In the Neuroscience ward, as I tried in vain to give him a bear hug to comfort him, I was unable to recognize my own dad. His pupils seemed to have turned upwards though his skin was still warm. *Where are you, dad? What would you say, if you could speak now?* I sat helplessly by his bedside asking questions of a man who had grown quiet in the last few years of his life.

Day after day, I would sit at his bedside, asking him question after question, without heeding the doctors' diagnosis. I would still wonder what it was he was thinking, feeling and remembering. I was in a state of stubborn refusal. I felt that something within him was still alive and sensing. His soul perhaps was making its rounds, in and out of his life and ours, reliving and taking stock of what he was and what he had become, frame by frame as if in a slide show.

How, I wondered, *would he see himself?* Overwhelmed by questions I had no answers to, I would fall into deep remorse and regret for not knowing enough of him as a child, young adult, husband, father and grandfather. As the Neuroscience ward darkened night after night, I would stay late by his side, compelled by a genuine desire to know my dad better and connect with him. Thus began my foray into my dad's eighty-odd years.

Chapter 2
WHO WAS MY DAD?

IN THE SILENCE OF the moments with my dad, in Tan Tock Seng Hospital, I couldn't help but see beyond and within his frail body. He was once a fifteen-year-old boy with an invincible spirit. He had the courage and audacity, at that age, to leave home for the biggest adventure of his life. What, I wondered, made a boy leave home and cross the seas for a land unknown to him? Was it aspiration for a better life, or desperation to leave what he may have perceived as a stultifying existence in a remote village?

My dad, Damodaran, named after Lord Shiva, the Creator and Destroyer of the universe, left Puthuval Veedu[3] in Anathalavattom, Kadaikavur District, Chirayankil, as a budding adolescent. Puthuval Veedu is the name of his ancestral home in the state of Kerala, close to the southern tip of the Indian subcontinent. You need to take a boat from the city of Trivandrum and cross a rivulet to reach the village. In other words, Puthuval Veedu is tucked away in lush coconut plantations and *padi* fields far away from what we would call civilization today. Puthuval Veedu was unknown to others, as was the little-known tiny island of Singapore.

Yet, unaccompanied by family members except for one acquaintance from his village who was returning to Singapore for work, my father boarded a steamship in pursuit of opportunities for a life that was beyond his imagination. My paternal grandddad, Kochupappu, whose name literally meant "little baby" in Malayalam, managed a tea plantation in Ceylon, the present-day Sri Lanka. (It was not unusual, in those days, for Malayalees in Kerala of Hindu,

---

3   *"new house" in Malayalam*

Christian or Muslim origin to name their sons Kuttan, Kutty or Kunghu. Curiously, those names all meant "baby" and were variations of terms of endearment, especially for male infants.) In spite of the implications Kochupappu carried in his name, he grew up to be a tall, handsome gentleman and fathered seven children. He struck a note with his long, aquiline nose and warm olive skin tone. For most of his married life, Kochupappu, my granddad, lived away from his wife and children, but sent them his earnings without fail for their upkeep. While he worked in Ceylon, his family managed the *krishi*, or agricultural land, that was passed down from his parents to him in Chirayankil. At home, his family grew mainly coconut and rice, and kept cows, goats and hens from which they made a living for themselves. At one of his routine visits home from Ceylon, my granddad's older sister proposed that her ten-year-old nephew, Damodaran, should leave home and come live with her in Trivandrum, the biggest town in Kerala State, some distance away from the village. My granddad's older sister was considered by the villagers to be a rich and capable woman who managed her family and circumstances well.

So, young Damodaran ended up going to a school of some standing in Trivandrum and excelled especially in Mathematics as he enjoyed mental calculations. Together with his cousins, he lived a life of comfort and luxury under his aunt's roof. My dad had very fond memories of his life under the charge of this tall and beautiful woman whom he admired for her *thandedum*[4]. She was capable, and above all she inspired confidence. Things were moving along swimmingly for four good years, but one day, sensing the growing distance dad felt from his family, his mother summoned her son to move back to the village and accept an offer as an apprentice at a tailoring guru's shop in Chirayankil. So, it was back to the village for young Damodaran. The vocation was thrust upon him.

---

4 *"capability and confidence" in Malayalam*

Back at home, on one fortuitous day during his sojourn at the tailor shop, the tailoring guru had to run an errand and left the premises under my dad's charge. The guru was gone for the whole day. In those hours, my dad was his own boss. The fourteen-year-old boy took the order to stitch a western suit for a male client, and audaciously, promised delivery the next day. He took the client's measurements, cut the cloth, and sewed a suit. It was his first solo attempt at creating a suit. It must have had a profound effect on his self-esteem and confidence. He was jubilant, and he couldn't wait to share his accomplishment with his guru.

Young Damo found the guru's response curious, though. It was lukewarm. The look of astonishment on his guru's face turned instantly into one of jealousy, borne perhaps from an unfounded fear of being displaced by this boy who he would have considered a young upstart. The guru, caught by surprise, was not aware that his apprentice was just as amazed. The young boy, however, was not allowed to bask in the light of such a feat. The tailoring guru dismissed the accomplishment and continued to give the boy menial tasks. For months, he was made to stitch buttons and buttonholes on shirts and suits. The repetitive nature of the task irked my dad.

But the suit fit and the client was happy. It was a watershed moment. For many days, my dad held the precious memory of the sweet victory, and turned it in his mind until the wheels of ambition were set in motion. He saw for himself that beneath the veneer of goodwill, life in the village was deeply ingrained in tradition and hierarchy. The lesson was clear: he could only depend on himself to grow and prosper. The taste of life in a bigger town, under the patronage of his wealthy aunt, may have fueled his dream to start his own tailoring business. But he realized, with some regret, that his dream was too big for this small village. He anticipated resistance from his family, who considered the apprenticeship to this guru of tailoring God-sent. They were very grateful, but my dad's spirit was on fire. He was impatient to make things happen.

Singapore, under colonial rule in the late 1930s, was touted to be a land of promise, but little else was known about it. My dad had friends, much older than himself, who lived and worked at the British naval base in Singapore. One such acquaintance was Vincent. Sensing the young boy's excitement and readiness to fly, Vincent encouraged the big move, offering to accompany dad and be his guardian in Singapore. All my dad needed now was enough money to get him across the seas.

His decision to leave for Singapore was met with unhappiness by his family. By this time, his father had stopped working and was devoting most of his time to prayer in a small temple he had erected some distance away from the family's main house. He would every morning resolutely bathe in the river, and then carry out prayers throughout the day which earned him the name *poocha sanyasi* meaning "holy fraud." In short, the villagers were skeptical of Kochupappu. In their eyes, he was a stranger who made little effort to be a part of their community. With his increased attachment to spiritual life, and detachment from domestic duties and responsibilities, it fell upon the eldest son, my dad, to support the family of five sisters and a brother. Hence their reluctance to let him go away. But it appeared that no amount of tears or emotional blackmail from his mother and sisters could stop the young boy from leaving the village. Young Damo stubbornly refused to give in to their plea. His father, ultimately, yielded and provided him with just enough money for the passage to Singapore. My dad left the shores of Kerala with nothing but a few items of clothing. The young boy was over the moon. He did not for a moment think that he was abandoning his family. He saw the move as an opportunity to provide the family with more, in the days to come.

So, in 1939, my father set sail on the SS *Rajula*, a troop and passenger ship of the British India Steam Navigation Company Ltd., starting from Madras (now called Chennai). The ship made its way to Nagapattinam, Penang and Port Swettenham before arriving safely on the shores of Singapore after eight days at sea. As many immigrants did during those times, he declared himself to be older than his fifteen years so he could qualify for employment in British Singapore where the naval base required coolies for various unskilled jobs. The word *coolie* originates from two South Asian languages. In Telegu it means "day labourer" and in Urdu, "slave." He would also have declared a fake birth date. For Hindus in Kerala, the date and time of birth were important in charting the astrological birth signs of the newborn baby. But after the birth, only the birth sign mattered, and the date of birth was ignored. Families would celebrate their children's birthdays according to the astrological sign. My father's astrological sign was *Bharani*. This meant that birthday celebrations under the sign of Bharani would be on different days from one year to another year in the Gregorian calendar. So he genuinely may not have remembered his date of birth.

What gave rise to his courage and audacity to have big, bold dreams that lay well beyond the ambit of a little village? *Vaashi* in Malayalam means the will and determination to succeed beyond all odds. It's a stubborn determination that does not take "no" for an answer, that drives one to overreach and break the boundaries of convention and cross oceans unheard of. Or perhaps the few years of good life at his aunt's home, in a big town, provided him with a vision of the kind of life he wanted to lead. It could have been that mental image that spurred him to go in search of a life which he thought would be unattainable if he were to remain in a village of old cronies who would dash a young man's dream.

On arrival in Singapore, he stayed with his cousin who became his official guardian. He did not have to wait long to start work at the British Naval Base—cleaning naval engines. It was messy work. Stubborn oil stains needed to be scrubbed at the end of each day. He hated it. He found little satisfaction in spanking clean, shiny engines, after having tasted the joy of creating something of beauty from raw materials. He quit the job and went in search of his dream. He was overjoyed to find work as an assistant to a tailor. He did this for a few years, but found little contentment in working for others. It is likely that, once again, he was left to carry out repetitive menial tasks which he abhorred. The spirit grew restless, and he yearned to recreate that moment when the suit fit the client. Time, he decided, was ripe for him to set up his own business. He rented a shophouse at 83, Kampong Bahru Road, from the Alkaffs, who were rich Arab merchants. My dad, who was no more than nineteen by now, set up his own suit and shirt tailoring business in these premises. He bought display cabinets, a Singer sewing machine and tailoring accessories. As the business grew, he hired a Chinese tailor to assist him. To supplement his earnings, he sublet all the extra rooms and extra space in the shophouse to mostly immigrants, like himself, from India. The location, being the hub of the city's growth, proved lucrative for business.

Young Damodaran made his dream come true within five years of landing on the shores of Singapore. His spirit was finally contented. He made enough income from creating suits and shirts to send money home for the upkeep of his parents and siblings. As a dutiful son, he did not miss a single payment. It gave him much joy to see his family happily settled in Chirayankil.

My dad was adaptable and assimilated very quickly into the local culture, and soon was considered a successful businessman by his relatives in Kerala. In Singapore, he had bachelor friends with whom he would get together for recreation. They would cook up a feast, have their beers and rejoice. They would go to the movies, Queen Elizabeth Park, Chinatown and New World Stadium for entertainment. He also took up bodybuilding. He lifted weights and kept himself lean and fighting fit. My dad did his own cooking in his bachelor days and became quite a connoisseur of food. He was never one to overindulge and give in to excesses. He acquired a taste for different cuisines—Chinese, Malay and Western—but Malayalee dishes remained his favourite.

My dad had built a fine life for himself, but one day he was greeted with unpleasant echoes from his village in Chirayankil. He received a letter from his younger brother, Renganathan. Wanting to attend university, his brother had apparently approached their rich uncle in Chirayankil for financial assistance, a loan perhaps. The uncle's response, "*Anna thoorunhe mathiri aadu thooriya okila,*" was as crude and vulgar as it was dehumanizing. The direct translation in English might leave one puzzled: "goats cannot expect to shit like elephants." It simply meant that it is foolish for goats to aspire to be elephants. Goats must remain goats. "But if you think you are that grand," sneered the uncle who was his mother's older brother, "go ask your brother in Singapore to support you." For my dad, it was a harsh and disturbing reminder of the childhood in Kerala that he had walked away from years earlier. My dad understood the humiliation to his younger brother's dignity and self-worth.

Renganathan needed financial assistance for four years to study at one of the top universities in Bangalore. It meant leaving home. In addition to the fees, he would have to pay for his room and board. It was a big financial commitment, but my dad agreed to help. It was a moment to be proud of. His younger brother would be one of the first to qualify for university in his family, and probably his village, too.

So, promise him, he did—to fulfil his dreams. Just as my dad inspired his younger brother to have big dreams, so was my dad encouraged to work extra hard in the coming years to send a sibling to university. He considered it a great honour and privilege. Every month, for four years, my dad sent more than half of his earnings to pay for Renganathan's fees, room and board. Upon graduation, Renganathan B.A. was offered a job at the Kerala Government of India Secretariat in Trivandrum, the highest echelon of state administrative structure. My dad would sing praises of his brother's achievements to his family and friends. Never once did he ask his brother for the money he had spent on his education, nor did he ever complain about how hard he had to work for it. He was proud to hear from his relatives and friends how well-respected his younger brother was in Trivandrum. Although Renganathan held a highly regarded position in government office as a district collector for many years, he was known for his humility and integrity. Over the years, my dad also helped finance the marriages of his older sister and three younger sisters.

For me, decades later, it was agonizing to watch my ailing dad in this state of conscious unconsciousness, not knowing where his spirit was or what it longed for. I had a vision of a little boy I hardly knew. There were no stories of childhood friends, the games that he played or the childish pranks he may have got up to. I thought with much regret, *Here lies a little boy who had to grow up all too fast to assume adult responsibilities.* Though he grew to be a strapping young man full of vim to make things happen, it saddened me that he hardly had a childhood.

Chapter 3
YOU CANNOT RUSH THE DYING NOR THE LIVING

ACHA LAY UNCONSCIOUS IN Ward A of Tan Tock Seng Hospital for what seemed like an eternity. The days grew longer as we wrestled with decisions about life support. We were dithering between life, death and what felt like a grey inconclusive area that left us depleted. Echoes of dad's loud wailing sounds reverberated wherever I went. I felt his presence everywhere in my apartment. It was as if his spirit longed for company, wanting to break the silence that had befallen our home after he suffered his hemorrhagic stroke.

The stroke had affected a large part of his right brain. The doctors once again prepared us for his death. He could go at any moment, they said. Then, a few days later, we were told that his condition had stabilized. The following morning, on his fifth day of hospitalization, the doctors performed a CT scan that revealed yet another stroke which affected the left lobe of his brain. I was told that his condition was critical. The doctors wanted us to stand by. They could be calling us any time, and I was to relay the message to the rest of the family. I went to bed with my mobile phone on my bedside table, ready to act. A week passed, then ten days, followed by a spasm of time with no end. Nothing happened. Impatient, I requested to see the doctors. To my surprise, they informed me that dad's condition had again stabilized: "He is ready to be discharged. You can take him home." My dad was still being fed through the tube that led to his stomach. He was suctioned from time to time when fluids built up in his lungs. They told me his brain was engorged, just as were his lungs, with fluids. This was a stabilized condition?

After discussions, the hospital counsellor advised my brother, mum and me to consider admitting him into Ang Mo Kio Community Hospital for intensive therapy. We agreed. For days, I did not hear from the hospital staff and it felt like months. Finally the nurses reported that Ang Mo Kio Community Hospital had reviewed my father's case, but rejected him on the grounds that his chances for rehabilitation were very slim. In the twenty-five days in Tan Tock Seng Hospital, I had strangely grown accustomed to the routine visits where I would sit silently by his bedside and let my thoughts wander as I communicated silently with my dad. Surrounded by nurses and doctors who regularly attended to him had given me the false sense of assurance that he would one day wake up from this paradoxical state of consciousness—conscious but not conscious. Hearing the nurses' words, cold and calculated, I felt let down, rundown and depleted.

A couple of days later, I was referred to a counselor who offered the family two options: we could take my dad home or we could send him to a nursing home. When the discharge papers and reports were drawn up, I realized that all along, my dad had been kept alive by eight different drugs which were administered daily for his heart condition, the stroke, the fluid retention and all the complications that arose due to the side effects of these drugs. This was yet another feat of medical science: the miracles that kept his heart beating while his brain was dead and the rest of the body wasted away. He was all skin and bones. He opened his eyes less and less as the days went by. I could feel his fatigue and pain, even as the nourishment went down the tube into his stomach. At times, he would gasp for breath and break out in cold sweat. The nurses would change him two to three times a day, sometimes within a span of a few minutes. He was completely helpless and hopeless, but I wished he would speak even if it was to complain about how uncomfortable or painful it was for him. I would have found solace in his voice and in his words. I would shake him gently and say, "Dad, Dad!! What are you thinking? What do you want? Do you need something? Just say something! Anything!"

There were times he would lie in his bed, sleeping, only to wake up and stare with wide-eyed wonder. His gaze was piercing, but he seemed to be looking through us and beyond us into space, as if something or someone was beckoning. Then, as if it was all too tiring, he would drift off to sleep once again. It was puzzling for me how the doctors could have concluded that he was ready to go home, when he still clearly needed constant medical attention.

One night, back home after the hospital visit, I was alone in the living room, packing my bag for the following day at work. In the silence of the late hour I was interrupted by a distinct cough just behind me. It was dad. It was so clear, it startled me. It was too close for comfort. I looked over my shoulder spontaneously, expecting my father to be standing right behind me. I looked around to see where the sound could have come from. Nowhere, really—the windows were shut and the neighbourhood was fast asleep. But his presence was everywhere. Then two days later, again in the quiet of the night after switching off the living room lights, I walked into my bedroom and got into bed, fatigued from the visits to the hospital, when I felt the air freeze around me. It got distinctly colder. Suffocated, I could feel the chill engulf my entire body while my husband, Manmindar, slept soundly beside me. Unable to move or scream, I lay in bed with my eyes wide open for several minutes until I composed myself. Again, I wondered if dad's spirit was restless and in search of something.

Disturbed, I spoke to my mum about the ways we could provide him with some respite. Some Hindu friends suggested that I leave a tape recording of the *Gayatri Mantra* running in a low soothing volume by his bedside. The Gayatri Mantra is a powerful prayer in Sanskrit believed to dispel pain and inspire spiritual awakening. We hoped for revival. We hoped for dad's soul to find peace. We hoped most of all for him not to feel alone. And it was not only my dad who was in need of comforting. The soulful mantra, accompanied by music in the background, provided me with solace at the end of a hard day at work as we arrived at the hospital ward. My brother and I had friends who were Christians, Buddhists and Hindus who would request to do prayers for my dad. Knowing how inclusive my dad was, both my brother and I were open to these expressions of care and love. All this was possible in the privacy of a single ward. We spent many a quiet moment with my dad. There were days when I would appear at the ward to find my husband, brother or mum sitting alone by his bedside. I believed that they, too, were communicating with him silently. One such day, my brother whispered to my dad that his wife, Lynne, and he were expecting their first child. My dad was the first to know. My brother believed that my dad was still with us. I believed that he was there with us, too, and that he rejoiced to hear these words, that he was listening.

Towards the end of his thirty-day hospitalization in the Neuroscience ward of Tan Tock Seng Hospital, my dad appeared in a dream. He looked sad and forlorn. In a soft voice he pleaded me to give him some water as his throat was dry. "Shali, vellam venam." I woke up horrified and shaken, convinced that his throat was indeed parched as he had been tube fed for almost thirty days now. When I told my mum and her older sister, aunty Letha, about my dream, they sighed with a knowing look: "We have to fulfill his wishes." The next day, we asked the nurse on duty if we could give dad some water. She gave us an incredulous look and muttered, "You know that is going to choke him to death, right?" Nevertheless, my aunt defiantly took a teaspoonful of water, wet dad's lips and pushed the spoon into his mouth when the nurse was away. My mum and I took turns doing the same. I felt consoled as I believed that I had fulfilled one of his needs. For me, it was more than a dream. It was real. Later that evening, I discovered from my aunt that we had performed the Hindu folklore ritual that takes place when someone is on his last dying breath. Water was considered the armistice for the soul to help it settle past issues or conflicts. My mum and aunt believed that my dad's soul was ready to be released from the body that had become a burden to him. I, however, wasn't sure though if my dad's soul was raring to leave us.

I had always professed vehemently that I would never send my parents to a home for the aged, but here I was, contemplating that very thing. It was the hardest decision to make. I consulted my brother, who agreed that we didn't have a choice but to send him to a nursing home. I thought about it and finally decided that perhaps we should take him to the Sree Narayana Mission Home for the Aged Sick where there were nurses and a medical doctor on duty. My good friend's sister was also a volunteer doctor at the Home. More importantly, I felt that I was placing my dad at the feet of the late Sree Narayana guru, whom he revered. The Home of the Aged Sick was also home to Sree Narayana Mission and its disciples. Prayers were carried out daily at the premises to keep alive the teachings of the late guru.

As my dad was already a life member of the Mission, the arrangements to get him admitted were swift. Now it was my turn to accompany my dad in the ambulance. This morning was unlike the frenzy my brother experienced that fateful morning when my dad first got sick. The traffic was smooth. No one seemed to be in a hurry. And there was no sense of urgency. In a strange way, it reflected my dad's condition that had stabilized. It was almost laughable: here was a man, still unconscious and still sustained through tubes, but apparently not battling for his life. For me, that journey from Tan Tock Seng Hospital to the Home of my dad's guru was like a dream. It was as if I was carrying out instructions from—I know not whom. I was simply doing. It was surreal. I was sure that dad would've wanted to come home with us, but, as in a nightmare, I could not change the course of that journey.

The family's trips to the Home for the Aged Sick were now less frequent. I would have wanted to be by his side more often, but as a teacher, wife, mother and daughter, my life could not stop to take heed of this difficult time. It was hurtling ahead, unimpeded by my dad's desperate calls. Tan Tock Seng Hospital had been ten minutes away from where both my brother and I lived, but the drive to the Home took us about forty minutes from Bukit Timah Road, where we lived, to Sembawang. Visiting ate up a good amount of time. I tried to visit him every other day while my mum called on him every day. It was difficult for my children, husband, and my brother to make regular trips to the Home because of school and work commitments. My brother's wife, Lynne, was also in her first trimester of pregnancy. It was a precious pregnancy for Lynne who was in her early forties. I told them that my dad would understand. These were helpless times. We had reached a stalemate. There were no more moves to be made. It was a period of waiting and wondering. We could only console each other to move on with our lives as there were many day-to-day responsibilities we needed to fulfill. These were perhaps the darkest days of our lives, as we could not know how long we could hang in there with our dad in his stabilized state.

    A tough part of the journey was arriving at the Home; I would greet the statue of the Guru at the entrance, before making my way past the vacant expressions on the faces of men and women, many of whom were Chinese, Indian and burdened. They sat in enclosed premises—some on wheelchairs, others on plastic chairs or wooden benches—staring into nothingness. And there was my dad in one of the rooms along with the withered old men, save one who looked middle-aged and well built. I wasn't sure what he was doing there. He looked neither old nor struck with some tragic ailment. He glared at us every time we walked into the room of eight residents. At the end of the room, in the corner by the window, was my dad, still feeding and breathing through tubes. Every now and then, he would shake us up with his loud guttural wail. I understood now why the middle-aged man sent us daggers every time we visited. The other residents were probably too tired of life to feel anything, let alone be bothered by my dad's loud protestations. They hardly looked up as we walked in; they lay on their beds, slumped and listless. My dad was obviously making his presence felt in the Home at least to one of the residents. I was glad that my dad wanted to be heard.

All this time, I kept my brother informed of my dad's wellbeing. One day, my brother called me to relate a disturbing dream he had had. He had dreamt of a mute boy we knew in our childhood in Kampong Bahru. He had a youthful look and hair that was thick, shiny and black, swept to the side with Brylcreem to keep it in place. His face was severely distorted on one side. His utterances were hardly audible. We never understood a word of what he said, though he would speak incessantly to all the boys and girls in the neighbourhood, as if we could hear and understand. In the dream, this voiceless boy, with whom we had lost touch after over twenty years, was desperately trying to communicate something to my brother. What was it? It made my brother wonder why he had that dream. It made me wonder, too: we were desperately trying to read into all our dreams and look for signs of what lay ahead of us.

A few days later, a framed wedding portrait of my mum and dad fell inexplicably off the dining room wall where it hung. The glass shattered, and the light brown wooden frame, that had withstood fifty years of handling, came apart at the joints and revealed the tiny nails that kept the picture intact. Shaken, I removed the glass pieces and saved the picture. When my mum, husband and I witnessed the mysterious event together, we looked at each other without saying a word.

Chapter 4
THE MARRIAGE

IN MANY A TRANQUIL moment as I watched my mum by dad's bedside, I wondered about their relationship. Like most Asian couples, they were not openly affectionate, though I could see how they drew strength from each other's presence all these fifty years or more. While dad lay helpless in his bed, I puzzled over what was going on in my mum's mind. She was mostly silent the entire period. What would she feel with his passing?

My mum was by my dad's side every day in spite of his frustrating lack of recognition and response. Presumably, he did not see her or feel her presence. He did not seem to respond to her, except for the occasional wail. Here were two people, one as helpless as the other, communicating silently. Just as my dad lay, perhaps, preparing the stage for his final departure from her, my mum was there with him, every step of the way, praying silently for his wellbeing. She was at his bedside every morning, and she would return at dusk. I did not succumb to my urge to ask her questions about what she was feeling because I knew that attaching words to feelings of intimacy and love would surely spoil what they shared, as man and wife. After all, they had been companions, in the full sense of the word; side by side, they raised a family for more than fifty years.

As I watched my mum and dad, I realized that in spite of their many differences, they were both fundamentally strong and resolute, and unwavering in their love and commitment to each other. What were the circumstances in which they met? It got me pondering on their relationship, and I wondered what my maternal granddad had seen in my dad that made him promise his twelve-year-old daughter's hand in marriage.

My maternal grandfather was a tall, debonair contractor in Butterworth who was well-respected in his community. He was also a counsellor and small-time physician whom members of his community approached for a resolution to their physical and emotional problems. As a contractor, much of the time his job took him to construction sites in different parts of north Malaysia, far away from the family. Like my paternal grandfather, my maternal granddad's name was *Kuttan*, a term of endearment which also meant "baby" in Malayalam. This poised and confident gentleman brought up his three girls and two boys with most of the luxuries of *kampong* life. Whenever he came home after a long stint away, he would bring sacks of *durians, mangosteens* and other rations of food that the family adored. They lived in houses with English furniture and record players, and were all sent to English intermediate schools, where English was the main language of instruction. The eldest daughter, however, was married at fourteen to the only son of a well-to-do family in Perak. *A tad too young,* one would've thought. The groom, many years her senior, was a well-known, talented cricket player in Malaysia, and prone to excessive drinking, they discovered a bit too late.

Life was good for my mum and rest of her family, until my mum's father discovered that he was ill. Tuberculosis was almost always fatal back then, and his condition worsened by the day. His younger brother, Ramakrishnan, an Assistant Superintendent of Police (ASP) in the Singapore Police Force, was overwrought by the news. Granduncle Ramakrishnan held his older brother in high regard because my granddad had thrown him a lifeline when he was in India by bringing him to Singapore to get him educated. The love and strong bond between the two brothers was evident when my granduncle visited his ailing older brother in Butterworth. My granduncle Ramakrishnan was unhappy with the medical treatment his older brother was receiving, and he insisted that the entire family move to Singapore to get his brother the best medical care. Persuaded by my granduncle Ramakrishnan, the whole family uprooted and came to live with him, his wife and five children. Notwithstanding the fact that ASPs in the day were appointed bungalow houses with many rooms, the gesture of goodwill was unprecedented. On arrival in Singapore, my granddad was hospitalized immediately, and arrangements were made for my mum, Indira and her younger sister, Prema, to attend St. Theresa's Convent Secondary School, while her older brother, Chitharanjan, attended Gan Eng Seng Secondary School.

Fated as it may have seemed, my granduncle's house in New Bridge Road was located ten minutes away from my dad's tailoring shop. When my granddad got a little better and was discharged from hospital, he would take walks with my grandma along the shophouses in Kampong Bahru. On one of the walks, curious to see a young man reading the Malayalam papers, they stopped to chat. My dad and granddad got to talking about Indian and domestic politics mostly, putting into motion a chain of events. Three months of regular walks and many visits later, my mum overheard a conversation between her parents. They liked my dad. "He is a decent hardworking man," they claimed. He didn't drink or smoke, and they felt that he would be a suitable husband for my mum. They approached my dad with a marriage proposal. My dad would've seen my mum walking to school with her sister because to get to St. Theresa's Convent from New Bridge Road where they lived, the sisters would have had to walk past my dad's shophouse.

My dad was happy with the proposition, but he said he could marry their daughter only after he fulfilled his obligations to his family in Kerala. "It would take approximately five years," he said. He had to wait for his brother to finish university and get his sisters—two older and three younger—married. My grandparents agreed to that arrangement. My dad then requested a photograph of my mother to send to his parents in Kerala, asking them for permission to marry my mum. They were happy to give him their blessings. Arrangements were then made for my dad's very first meeting with my mum, at my granduncle's house. My mum was in her room. She was twelve, a schoolgirl, and my dad, twenty-five. My dad entered the room, professed his intention, and asked my mum one question in Malayalam: "I would like to marry you. Are you happy to marry me?" My mum, who was not expecting such a straight upfront question, was taken by surprise. She blurted, in Malayalam, the first thing that came to her mind: "I am happy, if it will make my parents happy." My dad left the room calmly, though he was really elated with the answer.

In the days and months that followed, my maternal grandma, wanting her own independence and home, was not happy to be living under my granduncle's roof. She pressured my granddad to take the family back to her village in Palghat, South India. She wanted to be with her mother and siblings, all of whom lived in Palghat. Though my granddad was not happy to disrupt his children's education, he had little choice but to agree with Thangam, his good wife. So the family uprooted once again, except my mum's older brother.

For my dad, it would be a five-year wait. But he was unfazed. My dad was very keen to have my mum's hand in marriage, so before she left for Palghat with her parents and two other siblings, he gave her a gold ring as a present to show his commitment. He proved to be a patient, steadfast suitor. After her departure, he would write her letters and send her gifts. One such gift was a Parker fountain pen, with her name engraved on it. It read: "Indira Damodaran" in clear, bold letters to remind her of his devotion to her. My granduncle, Ramakrishnan, who was entrusted with the delivery of the Parker pen on one of his visits to Palghat, was, however, not too pleased with the gift. They were not yet married, but my dad had brazenly abandoned her maiden name for his. He quizzed my mum about the pen: "Shouldn't it be Indira Kuttan? Why is Damodaran being so presumptuous?" My mum shook her head modestly. But the gift was delivered nevertheless. This was in the third year of his five-year wait.

In Palghat, my mum had several suitors where she lived, one of whom was a doctor. My granddad could have easily gone back on his word and married her off to one of the many suitors in India, but instead he turned them all away. What did he see in my dad? There was a thirteen-year difference between them, and my mum was only twelve when she was promised to my dad. Besides, they were separated by a huge gulf of space and time! It is inconceivable to me how such an arrangement could have been made and met.

During the five years when he was betrothed to my mum, my dad would visit Pearl's Hill where my granduncle's family had moved, to pick up my mum's older brother, Chitharanjan, who stayed behind to pursue his Cambridge School Certificate. It was a weekend breather that turned into a delightful routine. My dad would treat him to sumptuous meals and movies. It was an outing that both looked forward to. My uncle was barely fifteen and my dad almost twice his age, but my dad knew how to treat this young man. My dad was generous with him, and indulged him at restaurants that were not just Indian but Chinese. He also took him to the movies. My uncle looked forward to being pampered and entertained by my dad, but it was also time away from his uncle's and aunt's strict upbringing.

When my mum turned eighteen, Chitharanjan, who was about twenty, made the journey to Palghat in South India to bring my mother back to Singapore. My dad was thirty-one and my mum, eighteen, when they got married in Singapore at the Sree Krishnan Temple in Waterloo Street in 1955.

My dad was enamoured by my mum. She had long, curly, shiny black hair, light skin and movie-star features. In Palghat, directors of Malayalam films approached my granddad with offers of film roles for her, but he rejected them. He knew the temperament of this daughter: my mum was shy, quiet and intense. She would brood for days on her own when despondent. She had always wanted to continue her studies, but the move from Malaysia to Singapore and then to India, disrupted her education. And now there was the marriage promise that was going to dash her dreams forever. Granddad offered his youngest daughter instead for film roles as she, Prema, was as beautiful as she was bold. She loved singing, dancing and play-acting. She knew that she was coveted for her looks. While the younger sister entered the film world and made her way to stardom with her first hit movie, "Neelakuyil" co-starring one of the prominent Malayalam movie stars, Prem Nazir, my mum learnt how to read and write Malayalam, Tamil and Hindi in her spare time.

It couldn't have been easy for my dad to bring such a beautiful young bride into such an eclectic environment. The stretch of post-war colonial shophouses in Kampong Bahru Road where we lived was flanked on the left by a coffee shop that sold *roti prata*, curry and rice, a provision shop that sold all and sundry, and a hairdressing salon. On our right was a barbershop. Beside the barbershop lived a nurse who used the shophouse as her residence, and then a car-tyre shop that was dark and grimy with engine oil, and old and new car and bicycle tyres. Next came a bar that provided endless drama; fights would erupt in the evenings between triad groups and Caucasian men over Asian bar girls. The fistfights were accompanied by *parangs* and knives. Often, they drew blood. And then, a few doors away lived a respectable Indian tailor with his six children and wife. They were staunch practicing Hindus who started and ended their day by singing *bhajans* together as a family.

Most of the small businesses were operated by men. It must have been nervewracking for my dad to bring his innocent bride into Kampong Bahru (literal translation from Malay language—"Village New"). My mum was sensitive. On arrival in her new home, she continued to brood, quietly lamenting her fate. Dad's pet name for mom was *poocha*, the Malayalam word for "cat," as she was soft and quiet. My dad would discover later that this *poocha* had a feisty side to her which he brought out by gradually gaining her confidence. While my dad probably felt like the luckiest man in the world, I think it might not have been easy for him around *poocha*. He treated her with the utmost care and respect, and was careful to protect her from the lecherous eyes of men. He had sublet all the rooms in the second floor of the shophouse to men who lived single lives, away from their wives in India. Realizing how difficult it was for my mum to live under such circumstances, my dad took it upon himself to shelter and safeguard her from any harm. He would do the marketing every day before starting work, and run all the errands. This arrangement made it unnecessary for her to ever leave the house on her own. She would only go out with my dad. My mum had been somewhat pampered by her own mum and dad. She didn't have to lift a finger with household chores, let alone cook in her home. Dad had to teach mom to cook from scratch, starting with the rice and moving on to the vegetables and meat dishes gradually. The period of adjustment must have been quite traumatizing for my mum, but my dad's patience and his *vaashi* or determination to provide my mum with the best helped them build their life together and trust in each other. His perseverance bore fruit. For many years, my mum would cook and my dad would do the taste test. He could tell what was lacking in any curry by just tasting it. He became her culinary guide and protector for life.

I was born in 1956, a year after their marriage. My dad had always thought he would go back to Kerala eventually because it was where most, if not all, of his family remained. But when I was born, he had a change of heart. He wasn't sure if Kerala would be the best place to raise a child, let alone a girl. My dad was progressive: he would've wanted to educate me, just as he had educated his younger brother. He had visions of me going to university and becoming a doctor or lawyer. This was every Indian parent's dream those days, for their sons at least, but for my dad it included his daughter. He was not chauvinistic. So, he decided to stay in Singapore for a longer term.

But my father's heart was always in Kerala. When I was about four months old, dad did what all good sons would: he took my mum and my infant self to Kerala to his village in Chirayankil to meet his parents and relatives. It was the first of my travels overseas. The ocean was choppy. My mum was seasick and confined to the cabin. My dad, I am guessing, took care of me most of the eight days during which we were exposed to the elements at sea.

It was customary for parents who originated from Kerala to make a vow to feed their infants their first solids before the deity, *Murugan*, at Pazhani. It was an offering of gratitude. My dad could've made such a vow, or it could've been our relatives in India who promoted the idea of taking a whopping infant to a Murugan Temple located some hundred and fifty metres above sea level to be fed her first solids. Whatever the motivation, my dad, accompanied by some of our relatives, hiked up the hill of six hundred and ninety-three dirt steps to reach its summit where the inner sanctum of the temple lay. It was an hourlong trek. My dad used to relate stories to my mum of how I grew heavier and heavier with every step, and how I shat a whole lot, on my way up to the temple. He was amused by the grossness of getting rid of my soiled cloth nappies as they inched up the hill. My mum, however, was spared. She stayed behind at the foothills of the temple because traditional Hindu customs exempted menstruating women from any kind of domestic duty, be it cooking, washing or even visits to the temple. It was a period of rest, and rest she did, away from the motley crew that was making their way to the summit with an infant in arms. I was fed my first morsel of solid foods (probably yoghurt rice) by a priest with a profound rice belly.

In my dad's village in Chirayankil, my mum was the talk of the town. Men, women and children, mesmerized by her beauty, treated her like a film star. Every meal was a feast. Unhappy with their own little sheds, they arranged for the "foreign return" family to stay in brick houses of friends who had graciously offered a bedroom and bathroom with flush toilets. If not for these conveniences, my mum would've had to travel a distance away from the main house on foot through the *krishi* (farmland) to an outhouse. There a bucket lay in a hole in the ground for visitors to do their daily business, big or small.

There were night soil carriers in the village whose sole job was to remove the reeking buckets at the end of each day. That trip to dad's village in Chirayankil would have confirmed his decision to remain and live in Singapore. It was clear to him that my mum would not have been able to live in the village.

In 1960, four years later, my brother Suresh was born. By now, my dad's business was doing better, but we still only had one bedroom, a living room, a little kitchen and a little patio to ourselves, on the first floor of our shophouse. As I grew up, my mum, brother and I slept in a king-sized bed in the bedroom, while my dad would sleep in the shop on the hard teak table that doubled as his work table where he cut and measured fabric for sewing. Every night, he would put a cotton sheet on the table and lie on it, covered with a blanket from shoulder to toe. He always slept face-up, on his back. And I am guessing he always slept well because he would wake up whistling like a lark. He may not have thought of this daily occurrence as a sacrifice. My mum would prepare a quick breakfast of half-boiled eggs or *thoshas*, and coffee, beaten to a froth with condensed milk, to kickstart his day. Dad looked forward to working, reading and listening to the news of the day to prepare for the debates he would have with the friends who never failed to drop in on him every day. That hard, chocolate-stained teak table is something that is etched in my memory. To me, it represents my dad's unassuming sacrifice. I wonder where it has made its way now.

Chapter 5
THE RELEASE

WITH EVERY VISIT TO the Home for the Aged, I felt a part of me crumble. I carried bottled-up guilt and regret which, over time, had made itself visible as the bags under my eyes. The busy work of preparing lessons and teaching worked on me like an opiate for my frazzled nerves. I tried to forget my pain by submerging myself in a sea of ideas. "Let's examine the issues," I would say, but my eighteen-year-old students who were aware of my circumstances would want to share moving memories of the final days of their own grandma or grandpa. With their stories, they relived the pain of having to watch a loved one suffer helplessly while the clock ticked away, oblivious of its hold on us. "But it will all be fine," they would say. "They are in a good place. They are in heaven with the angels." I wanted to believe them but I couldn't see an end to my dad's suffering. It remained dark with no light in sight.

One day, noticing how drawn and fatigued I looked, the principal of my school who was a Catholic Brother called me into his office for a chat. He already knew what was going on and had comforted me when my dad was first admitted into Tan Tock Seng Hospital after his stroke. But this time, he gave me a perspective that was strangely illuminating. He told me that my dad was preparing us for his eventual demise. He said quite candidly that this lull has been provided for us to express our love and devotion to him. It would help us to grow in strength and accept that he would be with us no more. I savoured his every word. But the solace I felt was fleeting. There were days when I would experience intense chest pains on my way to the Nursing Home. It felt like a cardiac arrest, but I was told by a good friend who had just lost her brother that it was grief that I felt. When you grieve, it is your heart, that organ behind your breastbone pumping blood, that feels the pain, I learnt.

Watching dad in that state of unconsciousness and not knowing for sure if he was suffering took a toll on all of us. But my Catholic Brother's prophetic words proved to be true. When the phone call finally came, after a month of agonising visits to the Home, at 2.10 in the wee hours of the morning on 2 March 2004, I seemed to be prepared. I listened calmly, strangely relieved. I even felt thankful. I rang my brother and gathered the rest of the family. The Home was quiet and inexplicably peaceful and cool at that hour, dimly lit by a couple of warm yellow lights. My good friend's sister who was doing her night shift at Alexander Hospital kindly agreed to certify his death. We decided the funeral would be at home, where we felt his spirit would be most at peace.

Our home, on the day of the wake, was radiant with red, white and yellow rose garlands and flowers placed in the open casket where my dad lay. Smoke from the burning frankincense formed a fragrant cloud over my dad as if to strengthen and purify him from all the earthly ills. He looked at peace and dignified, wearing his yellow silk *juba* and pants. Sympathy stands of yellow gerberas, white pompoms, and white and pink lilies from our colleagues flanked the coffin, while soothing sounds of *Shiva* chants filled the air. That night we kept vigil. Close relatives of my mum stayed awake and joined us in chanting prayers and keeping the oil lamp alive at the foot of the coffin. I learnt that evening from our close relatives that the light from the flame flickering at dad's feet would help his soul find its way to where we came from: our real home. If that was true, a part of me felt comforted. But I still couldn't be sure if he was ready to leave us.

At the wake, we were surprised to see my dad's friends and their children who had been regular visitors at my dad's tailor shop some twenty years ago. Our apartment, in those two days, was heaving with friends of dad's children, grandchildren and a son-in-law—all came to pay their respects and comfort us. There were also my students and friends from school, all of whom brought the warm *kampong* (village) spirit back to life. Many of my dad's friends were old and feeble, yet they came in remembrance of a friendship they once shared long ago, at a time far away, in a street called Kampong Bahru. They had since left the area to live in Housing Development Board (HDB) flats, private apartments, and houses all over Singapore. City Towers, where we now lived in Bukit Timah Road, carried a little of what was left of the old spirit of community from days bygone; helpers who had known my dad cried as if he was their own, and neighbours came to offer their condolences and deep sympathies. My dad used to take walks at least twice a day on the grounds of the condominium, so most people knew him more than they knew me, I suddenly realized.

For the funeral, the undertakers needed a picture of my dad to be enlarged and placed before the coffin. I went through the family photo album. There were pictures of my dad that we took during our family holidays to Australia, India and the United States. In all of them, I began to realise, he looked happy and excited to be in the midst of his family, exploring new places. He had the infectious smile of a pure soul who felt abundantly blessed. But one picture stood out. It was a blockbuster. It was the photo he took with my brother on graduation day from the Faculty of Law at the National University of Singapore. You could see a sense of pride and accomplishment on my father's face. He was beaming.

That picture of my dad radiated silently as we paid our respects and carried out the funeral rites at home. A respected member of my dad's community and her son presided over the funeral proceedings. They chanted hymns and mantras while each member of the family encircled my dad with offerings of flowers and prayers as a demonstration of love, to liberate his soul from the body.

After the ceremony the casket was closed. While I felt as if I was going through the motions, I could see my brother struggling with his feelings. He was subdued, not his usual lively self. He and my husband, the main pallbearers, carried the casket down a flight of thirty steps from the apartment. We were greeted by sunshine and a light drizzle as we stepped out. It felt dreamlike. It lifted our moods. We felt every drop of rain cool and warm against our skin.

At the Mandai Crematorium, there were no speeches, no eulogies or famous last words. Friends and family once again encircled the funeral pyre with their silent prayers, and they placed red roses and carnations on my dad, his eyes closed and seeming to be at peace. Afterward, my younger brother, as the only son, performed the last rite before cremation. My brother carried an earthen pot full of water on his right shoulder, which the priest struck with a sharp sickle. The blow created a neat hole from which water streamed. Carrying the pot, my brother walked around the casket thrice while my husband and son followed closely behind, waving the stream of water gently with the back of their hands towards the pyre. It was an act of purification; the body was now ready for cremation. Whilst it was the belief that these rituals were performed for the smooth transition of the soul to the next life, I couldn't help but feel that more than the newly departed, it was meant for his family and friends to help them acknowledge and come to terms with the loss of their loved one. The rituals helped us to express our grief and cope with the bereavement as we bid dad's soul a blessed journey.

The family chose to observe a mourning period of sixteen days as was customary and befitting the demands of urban life. Although we did not quite dress in sober colours (white or cream, as tradition dictated), the period of mourning was solemn. All of us were given to reflection. We had simple vegetarian food and refrained from consuming alcohol. My brother, additionally, did not shave. At the end of the sixteenth day, he looked like a *Sadhu* or holy man. He sported a beard and looked at peace with himself. This time was precious for the soul to receive as much love as it could from his surviving family and close friends. Hindus believe that the departed soul would still be in transition, roaming around, unable to detach itself completely from this life. So send our love, in prayers, chants and thoughts, we did, for dad's soul to find its way home.

The day after the cremation, we had to collect my dad's ashes. Traditionally, only male members of the family were allowed into the chamber, with the eldest male child carrying out the post funeral rituals. As the elder of the two children, I wanted to be there, too, to provide my younger brother with support. The ritual required my brother to handle the bones and ashes, as mantras were chanted, and place them in an urn. Watching the ashes and bones of my dad, pure white to grey, being sifted and examined, was unsettling to me. I felt a strange dizziness overcome me at the sight of what remained of my dad. Unfortunately, it did not send me crashing onto the floor, although that was what I wished. I desperately wanted to run from that dark chamber that was filled with smoke and the piercing smell of frankincense, but I couldn't. I was compelled to stay and feel in my bones the stark meaning of death. It struck me with its plainness... bare bones and ashes. *Is that it?* I thought to myself. Life seemed to be one long journey into the pyre.

While my brother placed the bones and ashes into the urn, the elderly gentleman who was leading the ritual stopped to take a quizzical second look at what looked like a white piece of bone. Evidently, something unusual had caught his eye. In a heavy and thick voice, he said he could see Sanskrit words carved on the frontal skull bone of my dad. While he was not entirely sure what the Sanskrit words meant, he said it indicated that he was a great soul or *atman* in Sanskrit. "I have never seen anything like this," he muttered in Tamil. My brother and I looked at each other incredulously. Though we did not for a moment doubt that my dad was indeed a great soul, we couldn't quite fathom the full import of what he said. It was too much for us to process in that moment. Afterward we spoke about it briefly, before taking the ashes to be dispersed into the sea in accordance with the belief that submerging the ashes, especially in seawater, helped the soul detach itself from concerns of this world. We wished my dad a peaceful journey.

Part 2

Bereavement

Tear ducts are dry.
Parched,
I struggle,
With guilt, regret and anger,
Trapped between knowing and not knowing,
I am unable to grieve
And let go.
The angst builds in the chamber of life
Ready to cut off the air.

Like a bolt shot from the skies
Memories, lived and loved,
Come gushing,
Breaking down the walls.
Flooding, the tear ducts well
And flow as night falls
Into fortified pools.
I shut my eyes.
I give in to dreams, breathing.

Chapter 6
MOURNING. GRIEVING. REFLECTING.

A COUPLE OF WEEKS after dad's passing, my aunt, who was a Sister with the Brahma Kumaris, a religious organization teaching mind-body meditation, conducted prayers for the smooth ascent of my dad's soul to the next realm. The prayers were attended by close relatives and friends. During the prayers, we were required to focus on a point of light on a white wall and pray for my dad's soul to rest in peace, while the rest of the Sisters meditated on my dad's smooth passage. During the entire prayer, I cried uncontrollably. My emotions surprised me. My tears were unstoppable. It was as if a dam had opened its floodgates. Though I was saddened by my dad's passing, until then I had remained seemingly stoic, attending to my duties and obligations with a heavy heart. There had been no tears. Strange as it may seem, I never realized how much I loved my dad until those prayers commenced for the smooth passage of my dad's soul. At the end of the prayer, the Sisters told us that they had a very clear vision of my dad's soul being surrounded by light during their meditation. "He has reached the source," they uttered knowingly. The thought that he had detached himself from us and found peace gave me some sense of comfort and closure. But for me, it threw a distressing spotlight on the bond between a parent and child. I wondered what it was all about.

Dad's passing made me ruminate on his experience with the loss of his own parents. They were separated by oceans of time and space. He, in Singapore and they, in Kerala. How did he feel? Was he devastated? When his dad passed away, I was still a toddler and too young to remember. But according to my mum, on the day he received news of his dad's death in Kerala, he betrayed little emotion. He read the telegram and continued working in his tailor shop. He seemed detached. He had left home as a budding adolescent whose father was away, working in a different country most of his life. So, it should come as no surprise if he had felt nothing. But it's a parent, one to whom you owe your existence. It is not easy to feel nothing. My dad did not confide in my mum, though he had been married to her for a couple of years. He was solemn. What did he experience? Did he suddenly feel the weight of his responsibilities grow heavier on his shoulders? Though he had been already playing the role of a patriarch to his family in Kerala, he may have felt that things were different somehow. He was now the head of two households; one in Kerala, and one here in Singapore.

But I remember distinctly the day he received news of his mother's demise. I was nine. My dad had opened his shop, as usual. Opening up required him to remove many narrow rectangular planks, painted blue, that stood in front of the closed shop. As he removed the sky blue planks one by one, a lizard jumped out from one of the gaps above, and fell right smack in the middle of his head. Though my dad was not usually superstitious, he was upset enough to relay the incident to my mum. According to *Palli Shastram* or "Lizard Astrology," which predicts the effects of lizards falling on different parts of the human body, the event portended the death of someone close. I remember that his eyes looked like brimming wells, deeply disturbed, as he had learnt a month before that his mother was very sick. My dad had just sent her blankets and rations of food items to comfort her. Included in the package was a gift of a beautiful Kashmiri woolen and silk shawl which she had said she loved.

A few hours after the ominous episode with the lizard, a telegram arrived from dad's younger brother, Renganathan: "Mum died peacefully." My dad put all the planks back together and closed his shop. He looked visibly distraught, and remained solemn the entire day. There was nothing much to do but mourn his mother's death in silence. As her eldest son, he would have been the one to perform the funeral rites, but time and space did not allow it. In those days, you couldn't fly to reach your destination within a day. I consoled myself that mother and son were probably united in spirit. I wished that he, too, could have taken comfort in that belief. How I wished I could've consoled him. I realised I was just as private in my mourning as my dad. As the days passed into months, I would quietly reminisce my childhood days with my dad.

A few months after the *Athma Shanti Pooja* or prayers for the smooth passage of my dad's soul were carried out, I had an unnerving dream about my dad. He stood beside me looking rundown and despondent. In a soft voice that was hardly audible he murmured, "You never celebrated my birthday." Startled, I woke up sobbing as if he had come back in person. How true, that we never did, not once, in his eighty-odd years, celebrate his birthday. But I rationalised that it was because we didn't know his date of birth, and neither did he. The date that was declared in his identity card and passport was not his. We took it for granted that he didn't care to celebrate his birthday, although we did it for every other member of the family, including my mother, without fail. While I told myself it was only a dream, I couldn't help but feel pangs of regret and remorse, in spite of the excuses I conjured. I was at my most fragile, and I would tear up easily at the thought of my dad. For months, I couldn't speak about him without crying. I spent much of my time feeling hopelessly guilty. I went through moments of our time together, when he lived with us in City Towers. These memories were tucked away in different rooms in my mind, and I would spend long hours in each, trying to connect with my dad and get to know him better.

When my daughter was born, my dad and mum had moved in with us, from the prewar shophouse where we were raised in Kampong Bahru, to our two-bedroom apartment in City Towers. As full-time working parents, my husband and I needed my mum and dad to be around to keep an eye on the baby, though we did have a live-in domestic helper to take care of the household chores. City Towers was close to the hustle and bustle of Orchard Road and a leisurely ten-minute walk to the heart of the city. What I liked best about the apartment was its high ceilings and long, spacious balcony that overlooked old majestic trees with luxurious branches shading the inhabitants of a timeworn bungalow from the city lights. Beyond the bungalow and wooded area rose the sky, revealing the cityscape. From the apartment we could gaze at the skyline of tall buildings without being touched by its buzz. The old bungalow house with sandblasted walls, no longer white but speckled with age spots, creepers and fungi, nestled in the mature overgrown foliage. It was a sight to behold from our balcony. The apartment was lovely. I had always assumed that my dad was happy living with us, but now as I lay reminiscing, I had my doubts.

As the family grew, we couldn't keep the chaotic pace of city living out of our lives. We got busy developing our careers, looking into the children's school and their extracurricular activities like tennis, cricket, swimming, rollerblading and cycling. We were having to keep up with a frenetic pace, mostly chauffeuring our children from one activity to another after school and on weekends; our lives were brimming over with to-do lists.

To escape from an overcrowded home, my husband and I would go for long walks along Balmoral Road, past Stevens Road and up Anderson Road. We would sneak out for *Teochew* porridge at the Shangrila Hotel in the evenings. My husband and I also had the luxury of weekly date nights. We would happily flee from our responsibilities, taking comfort in the thought that the children were safe with my parents watching over them. I wondered if my dad, too, had moments when he would have wanted to take long walks on his own or with my mum.

Having lived independently in the shophouse in Kampong Bahru all those years, how did he feel about living in City Towers with us?

Did he feel restricted? Was he comfortable having to live with babies, crying and puking, and us, young parents, green and hyper-reactive, when he should have been relaxing in a quiet and peaceful space, having, "been there and done that"? After all, his adult life began at the tender age of fifteen. Didn't he deserve a break from it all?

Looking back at the time mum and dad lived with us in City Towers, I thought to myself that he had fought to remain relevant. He would volunteer to run errands and do the marketing and grocery shopping for the family every week. He would take the bus mostly, and sometimes walk to Tekka market, enthusiastic to play a role in our lives. He also loved it when we entertained friends and family at home, as it gave him an opportunity to talk to us. Like a connoisseur, he would do the food tasting after my mum cooked the dishes. It gave him great joy. But the conversations our guests had with my dad would not go beyond the respectful niceties. We were young. We were in our prime. We had careers that absorbed so much of our time, and children who took up the rest. There were issues and problems we shared with our friends. We spoke about politics, parenting woes and insecure bosses who made our lives miserable. There was so much happening in our lives. My dad would've loved to have joined us in these conversations, just as he once had with his own friends.

As I mourned his loss, it dawned on me that he had always held strong views that he expressed boldly with conviction, and the curtains had perhaps closed in on him before he could make his exit. There were no longer his friends who would stop by his tailor shop for animated conversations about Indian politics, and of course Lee Kuan Yew's governance. There were no longer the fiery political rallies in the Tanjong Pagar constituency, where he never failed to take us, as he was a proud supporter of the Peoples' Action Party (PAP). There were no longer the cries of *Merdeka!*[5] *Merdeka! Merdeka!* that packed a punch, raising goose bumps and dreams for a better Singapore. Those were dramatic and empowering times, gone.

---

5   *Merdeka!—a cry for independence and freedom in the Malay language*

Chapter 7
KAMPONG BAHRU DAYS IN THE '60S AND '70S

THE EXPERIENCE OF LOSING my dad took me to his world like the tide that comes and goes for short visits to the shore. I wondered what made it easier for him stay in Singapore to build a home for himself and his family as an immigrant. I wondered what it would have felt like in Singapore without his parents, siblings and a whole village of people he knew intimately. It couldn't have been easy coping with homesickness. Just as there was a clear motivation to leave Kerala, what contributed to his strong sense of belonging to Singapore? There were so many questions I could've asked him to get to know him better. But I never did.

I recalled the neighbourhood of my childhood, and the prewar colonial shophouse in Kampong Bahru Road. We lived in one of the several brick shophouses connected by a five-foot way starting from the end of Neil Road and located near the Sepoy Lines Post Office, Singapore General Hospital, Malayan Railways and the Singapore Harbour Board. At the end of the row of shophouses were what looked like sheds, with red zinc roofs and zinc walls about seven feet tall, corroded and bent with age, and on the verge of collapsing. All you needed was a gust of wind to send bits of the roof and wall clanging. We hardly knew the people who lived in these houses. But we knew that cleanliness and personal hygiene meant something to them, because they would boil their clothes in a big pot that sat precariously on a charcoal stove in front of their homes facing Blair Road, a slip road off Kampong Bahru Road. Most of the time, the inhabitants kept to themselves but would occasionally emerge to dry their clothes on a clothesline erected in front of their houses.

Who were my dad's friends? Many of them who stopped by the shop, sometimes for hours to yarn about Indian and world politics while he continued to pedal away on his Singer sewing machine, were mainly Malayalees, Ceylonese and Tamils who held administrative positions at the Singapore General Hospital, Harbour Board or Malayan Railway. In the 1960s, administrative staff in these organisations were provided accommodation for their families in the vicinity of the places where they worked. Medical dressers and hospital assistants, for instance, lived in Hospital Quarters which in those days were like townhouses. Likewise, families of employees of the Malayan Railway and Singapore Harbour Board lived in walk-up apartments. Living in Kampong Bahru provided my dad with a network of like-minded friends, mostly men who had come to Singapore with their wives and children in search of a better life.

I used to hear my dad's voice rise and fall in excitement, and his laughter ripple through the narrow corridor of our shophouse to reach the bedroom, living room and kitchen, and the courtyard which was our living space. His friends provided him with many hours of entertainment for his mind and spirit while he worked. They obviously enjoyed the conversations they had with my dad as much as he did. I wonder now how these working men had so much time to spend at my dad's tailor shop during office hours.

I used to catch snippets of my dad's conversations, especially when they reached a crescendo. I listened to him chiding his friends for not applying to be Singapore citizens, and instead deciding to return to Kerala with their families. He thought it was a grave mistake because the opportunities for growth were so limited in Kerala. "Here, in Singapore, we have the luxury of choice," he would say, "and we are free from the stultifying effects of bureaucracy." Singapore, he would say, encouraged individual enterprise as the overheads were low and the government made it easy for people to start their own businesses without having to bribe government officials and go through oppressive red tape. He was a great advocate and spokesman of the Peoples' Action Party. But many of his friends left Singapore, especially when the British withdrew their military forces from the Singapore naval base in the '70s. They felt it spelled doom for Singapore's future. Those who returned to Kerala were the ones, presumably, with connections in India. They had a better chance of wielding power in their homeland. Some others who had jobs in the naval base were given opportunities to become British subjects. They left for the United Kingdom but my dad stayed in Singapore, in the midst of the flux, confident that they were wrong.

Singapore in the '60s must have felt as if it was at the centre of the universe, being strategically located at the crossroads of east and west. The world arrived at our doorstep, every day. The radio blasted local and global news, and Malayalam, Tamil and Hindi songs filled the hallway throughout the day. My dad would not miss the news for anything. He listened to the Tamil news that was broadcast on radio thrice a day. When the news was broadcast we had literally to hold our breaths. It was a priority. He was intense when he listened to the news. He would, additionally, read every single page of the *Malaysia Malayalee*, a regional newspaper, and *Maadar Bumi*, a Malayalam newspaper that brought news from Kerala. In his conversations, I would hear the names of politicians, whom he clearly admired, being bandied about. I listened to how Egypt's President Nasser outwitted the British to take over the Suez Canal. My dad seemed to applaud Nasser's political savvy in forming an alliance with the Russians. Perhaps influenced by my dad, I too became a fan of the Kennedy brothers, and was stunned when they were assassinated. Each time, I moped for days, as if I had lost a close member of my family. My dad was also an ardent supporter of the Congress Party in India, and the Nehru family. As a Gandhian enthusiast, dad had a portrait of the Mahatma hanging on the wall. My mum was influenced to read

Gandhi's autobiography when she was expecting me, hoping that, I too, would follow in the path of non-violence and peace. These were empowering times for my dad.

    Mourning the loss of my dad took me to my own childhood days and the lives we led then. I began to recalibrate and focus on how he was always there for us, though he seemed to be preoccupied a lot of the time behind the radio, newspapers or his sewing machine. My parents worked hard from eight to eight from Mondays to Saturdays, but on Sundays, they took a break. My dad was a different man on Sundays. He looked less intense. There was a time devoted to work that he enjoyed, but there was also a time to take a break. He would take us to Queen Elizabeth Walk. We would walk the stretch of the esplanade, have fun in the gardens and soak in the sea air. It was truly relaxing for everyone. My brother and I would run around and play. Afterward, we would often end up in Chinatown for a bowl of fish ball noodle soup, a welcome change from the curries my mum cooked. Sundays were also devoted to the cinema. We would go to Ciros Theatre in Telok Blangah Road or Rex Theatre on Serangoon Road to watch Hindi and Tamil movies, and the occasional Malayalam movie when it was screened in Singapore.

    I was precocious as a child. It was perhaps my way of getting my dad's attention. At one and a half years, right under my dad's nose I snipped a kitten's ear with his tailoring scissors that I found on a chair. If I hadn't bawled at the sight of blood, my father would've continued with his work, oblivious. At four, I walked into the barbershop beside my dad's tailor shop, and decided I would try my hand at hairdressing. I must have been convinced that it was no mean feat, so I snipped off my hair here, there and everywhere until it left several bald patches on my scalp. My dad was livid. He shouted at me, and my mother cried. The barber was sheepish, and so was my dad. They couldn't explain how I had escaped their gaze. I had to shave my head entirely because with the bald patches I looked like someone afflicted with scalp disease. I wore a scarf for months—in shame. Every time I did something naughty, my mum would blame my dad for being inattentive. But my dad was always around.

In my primary school days, I knew how to get my way with my dad. There were times when I wanted something and I would find the courage to ask him directly, as if it was a matter of urgency. One time, I wanted to go to the Orchard Cinema to watch "Mary Poppins" with my classmates and teacher. My dad's response was stern. He practically glared at me. He wanted to know why I had to go. What about my homework and studies? I told him I had to write a review on "Mary Poppins." I would cry, and of course my dad would give in. It was easy that way. He didn't like to see us unhappy. I was actually excited about riding on the first escalator that was introduced at the cinema. That was worth the tantrum. The escalator experience was great! It felt like a roller coaster ride. We rode up and down the escalator, squealing with excitement.

The other time he gave in to my tantrums was when my mum told me that my dad would sew me a new dress for my birthday as he normally did. I remember looking forward to the dress, but the afternoon came and went and there was no sign of a dress. I asked my mum what had happened and she said that my dad was trying to meet a client's deadline. So I lay on the wooden bench in the corridor between our bedroom and the shop, and I cried all afternoon. I chose the spot because I knew that my dad would be able to hear my sniffles. By the end of the evening, I managed to squeeze my dress into dad's agenda. There was never a dull moment for my parents.

The village where my dad grew up, in Kerala, would have been a somewhat safe and sleepy haven with nothing much happening from day to day except births, deaths and weddings, so my dad would have found Singapore complex because it was primed for economic growth, teeming with immigrants in search of better opportunities to eke out a living. This would have meant different things to different people. While most would have been driven by the need to survive and provide in honest ways to sustain themselves and their families, there also would have been those driven by unscrupulous character to make a quick buck at the expense of others. Singapore in the '60s was well known for its secret society activities and gangsterism.

So, the neighbourhood was united by the fear of secret societies and gangsters who stalked small business owners for protection money. Loan sharks would leave the head of a pig, bludgeoned and dripping in blood, at the doorstep of someone who defaulted on his payments. Thus, there was then a need for small business owners like my dad to protect their livelihood and loved ones. Everyone had to stand united against a common bully, and I think a sense of being part of a community was born then, in these people. There was camaraderie. All those who had similar goals of living in peace and harmony stood alongside each other. Barriers between the Gulams and the Alsagoffs, and the Tans and Damodarans, became grey and greyer. Nobody envied the Gulams, who lived in a three-storey house, because they still lived like everyone else in the neighbourhood even though they had money and property. Nothing distinguished them as special on the face of it. We ate well and dressed well. Food passed from one household to another, regardless of race or religion. We knew not to serve our Muslim neighbours pork or Hindu neighbours beef. Most of the Chinese ate everything, contributing in even greater ways to the spirit of community.

Our neighbourhood was multi-religious, multi-racial and multi-lingual. We had Malay, Chinese, Indian and Eurasian neighbours who became friends of the family. There were Muslims, Christians, Buddhists, Taoists and Hindus. My mum and aunt went on dates with their Chinese, Malay and Indian girlfriends. They would dress up in each other's ethnic outfits—*sarees*, *Punjabi* suits, *baju kurung*, *kebayas* and *cheongsams*—to take pictures at one of the photo studios in Tanjong Pagar Road. My parents' old photo albums are rich with posed pictures shot by professionals. It didn't matter if some of the neighbours were rich owners of businesses, or others like us who lived from hand to mouth. These women were celebrating life's riches; they enjoyed the friendship and companionship through their appreciation of different cultures. To put it simply, the diversity provided colour and fun in their lives. They were unhampered by differences in language, religion or ethnicity because their smattering of English and Malay went a long way in creating bonds.

While some of the women in the neighbourhood celebrated their friendship, there were many men in the neighbourhood who led lonely lives. These men were mostly immigrants from India who had left their wives and children to seek a livelihood in Singapore. They lived like bachelors, but were deprived and bound by duty to send most of their earnings home. Unlike my dad, they did not have much recreation in their lives except to chew betel leaf with white lime and areca nut which left permanent red stains on their teeth. They would cook their own meals, and seemed to enjoy talking about their lives in the villages in South India. But what they loved most, I think, was the dignity and self-worth that came from working hard. They were providers, at the end of the day. There were mouths to feed back home and that was that. There was nothing else to concern themselves with.

We valued each other's skills and strengths. We needed the barbers, the tailors, the cooks and the cobblers. And we needed, most of all, for the rich to remain rich to buy our goods and services. We wished everyone well. The children of some of the rich businessmen in our neighbourhood didn't do so well in school, as formal education did not play a significant role in their lives. They would join their family businesses once they came of age. But there were exceptions. One of the girls, a daughter of an Indian Muslim businessman who owned several commercial and residential properties in Kampong Bahru, was sent to England for her studies at nineteen. She would always come by our home for a meal during her vacation, with several stories about her love for horseback riding and how she broke her nose when she was thrown off a horse. We loved listening to her because she spoke with a British accent. Years later, she met the love of her life at college. He belonged to Malaysian royalty. All of us in the neighbourhood were invited to the wedding. It was a grand affair that was celebrated over many days. For children of small businessmen, like myself and my brother, education was a priority. Our parents ensured we excelled at school and learnt to speak and write good English, because it was perceived to be the only means to better your lot in life. In our minds, everything evened out eventually. As children, we didn't feel the social divide, and maybe neither did my dad, because he did what he had to, at his own pace and time. He was not a man in a hurry trying to outwit others to get ahead of the pack. He believed simply in an honest day's work.

Despite the harmony we enjoyed in our diverse neighbourhood, in July of 1964, when I was eight years old, one of Singapore's worst racial riots occurred over *Mawlid* to celebrate Prophet Mohammad's birthday. A religious procession attended by twenty-five thousand Malay Muslims was planned to take place from the Padang to Geylang. We heard stories from my dad about how the clashes between the Chinese and Malays during the procession had led to many casualties, and how twenty shophouses in Geylang and Jalan Eunos were razed to the ground, and how there were fears that the violence would spread all over Singapore. Curfews were imposed to contain the riots, and schools were shut. To us children, this meant we had more time to play and sneak into each other's homes, unseen by the soldiers who paced up and down the five-foot way. But many of the Chinese, Malay, Indian and Eurasian parents in our neighbourhood remained calm. They did not allow the communal violence to get to them. My dad would tell us, as a matter of fact, how one of his friends, a cameraman, was caught in the midst of the riots as he tried to take photographs. He was beaten with a *parang* and sustained head injuries. But he escaped death and was taken to the hospital in time. Like my dad, no one displayed signs of paranoia in the neighbourhood. There was a recognition that we needed each other to protect the sense of community that had been cultivated over the years. Nobody took it for granted. Since such wisdom prevailed amongst our elders, we were spared the ugly possibilities of communal violence erupting in our own backyards. We stayed indoors during the curfew, but business was as usual otherwise while men in jungle green paced up and down the five-foot way, in front of our homes, carrying their imposing rifles. We felt safe.

Chapter 8
THE MODEST ENTREPRENEUR

WHEN MY DAD RETIRED from his tailoring business, he had to give up his shophouse in Kampong Bahru. I remember having to make decisions about what to keep and what to toss. My dad wanted his Singer sewing machine of more than twenty-five years and the accompanying chair, scissors and tape measure. I think he had plans to keep some of his favourite clients by sewing at home where we lived in City Towers. That day, I gifted myself with a piece of my dad's tailoring furniture— a brown teak cabinet with glass sliding doors, about two meters in length and two meters in height. He had used it to store paper cuttings of his client's garments and the completed *cholis* or blouses. He had the cabinet specially made in the '60s to fit the right sidewall of his shop. I loved the dark chocolatey cabinet as it was well-aged to reveal its wood grains. I made arrangements for it to be moved to our apartment in City Towers and turned it into a bookshelf. My dad was quite amazed. Today, the five shelves in the cabinet display a thousand paperbacks that my husband and I have read over the years, alongside the literature books that I had studied at university and taught at junior college. The solid piece of teak furniture is one of the few memorabilia from my dad's tailoring business that I have treasured. It never fails to evoke questions and conversations from our guests.

My father was a true entrepreneur. He had the vision and flexibility to make swift changes to his business in order to keep up with the local scene. He understood that he had to make a transition from men's shirts and suits to women's wear because the late '60s and early

'70s saw the mass production of ready-to-wear men's shirts that were easily available in stores and even night markets. And with the rising cost of custom-made clothes, it didn't make sense for working-class men to spend their hard earned money on custom-tailored shirts when cheaper alternatives were available. Western suits, on the other hand, were exclusive garments affordable only to the well-heeled who made up a small percentage of the population. With changes in the global market affecting the average local consumer, my dad decided that it was no longer lucrative to carry on as a men's tailor.

Living in Kampong Bahru, he also realized that there were many more women with the means to keep up with fashion and spend their money on tailored clothes because they had full-time jobs mostly as nurses, clerks, secretaries and teachers. Whilst men's and women's western clothes were being mass manufactured, ready-to-wear *saree* blouses, called *cholis,* had to be custom-fitted if they were to look good on any *saree*-clad woman. Dad realized there was money to be made tailoring *saree* blouses.

Saree blouses or *cholis* were separate pieces of clothing worn with *sarees*. *Choli* blouses flattered the feminine physique because they were cropped at the midriff. They had to be stitched to perfection to fit the body snugly to accentuate the curves. Along with my mum, dad started then to reach out to his friends' wives first. Many of my dad's clients in the beginning were mostly nurses, doctors and wives of medical staff (because the tailoring shop was located near the Singapore General Hospital), and teachers (who taught in the many neighbourhood and mission schools in the vicinity of our shophouse). They would normally bring the blouse piece attached to all six yards or five-and-a-half metres of a *saree* to have it stitched. It would take my dad about an hour and a half to stitch a blouse.

His clientele soon grew exponentially through word of mouth. The ladies were also very comfortable with my mum taking their measurements in the privacy of our bedroom. Many clients would hang around for some sweet, black Lipton's tea whisked with condensed milk, and a chat in the dining area that doubled as the living room, facing a little courtyard and kitchen. The ceiling was double stacked, creating a sense of space in a small area. It was a warm, cosy space that provided the ladies with many hours of entertainment.

A number of my dad's clients were young modern women who would request that the necklines of their blouses plunge both at the front and back. Some would request spaghetti strap blouses. My father would always oblige, with a straight face. For him, these were bodies that needed to be custom fitted. I have never known him to betray any emotion or judgment. I remember a woman complaining to him about tailors who had messed up her *saree* blouses because they fit either at the waist line or bust line, but never both. She was a "D" or "E" cup and had a disproportionately slim midriff. Another had a prominently hunched back which required a special cut for a good fit. In all these special cases, my dad had to do his magic so that women of different shapes and sizes could look their best wearing a *saree*.

Then there was a middle-aged principal of a school, of Ceylonese descent. She was a regular visitor. She was immaculately groomed. Her *saree* was always neatly tied up with a brooch. She loved to chat with my mum, not just about fabrics and the fashion of the day, but about her sons who were of marriageable age. She would discuss their girlfriends and worry about the match. Many of the clients would pour their problems out to my mum. They became my mum's bosom buddies. Before long, we would be invited to their homes for lunches and dinners, and my mum would reciprocate by cooking up a feast for them at our shophouse. It made for a warm and comfortable liaison.

How did my dad keep up with trends in Indian fashion clothing for women? My dad was quite skillful and astute! He knew how to transfer his tailoring skills to create new garments, and he always met clients' needs. Women, young and old, came to the shop with clothing designs they had seen in magazines like *Femina*, a publication from India for modern Indian women by modern Indian women. He would never say "no" to creating something new. Other clients would bring their own designs sketched on pieces of paper. He was fearless and always had faith that he would be able to meet the client's wish. If he was fearful of botching up the job, he made sure no one knew. Once he cut the fabric, there was no turning back, but he took the risk and kept up with fashion trends set by Bollywood and Tollywood.

My childhood days were thus filled with colourful textiles. I loved the touch of Kanchivaram Silks, Benaris Silks, Kashmir Silks, organzas and cottons. Some were richly embroidered with *zari* or gold and silk threads. My dad would lay these fabrics on the huge teak worktable which was the size of two eight-seater dining tables. He would look at his measurement book, then chalk the lines directly onto the fabric using his wooden ruler and tape measure. He would then cut the fabric and stitch the pieces together to create *saree* blouses on his pedal-driven Singer sewing machine. He must have done all his calculations mentally before he stitched the *choli* blouses.

Some years later, after a trip to India, my father introduced the bra-cut *saree* blouse. The cups of the blouse fitted like a brassiere to further enhance the feminine curves. It was all the rage, but as this garment required skill and more time to complete, it was more expensive. Most of his clients were generous, but there were some hagglers who would try to squeeze every penny out of my dad. Annoyed, he would mutter under his breath how it was backbreaking work, but give in he would, as he had little stamina to quibble with these women. His time was precious for his other pursuits: reading and listening to the news.

One day, one of his female clients, an Indian classical dancer, made a request for him to stitch her a *Bharatha Natyam*, or classical Indian dance costume, because she was performing at the Victoria Theatre in Singapore. My dad, who had never before stitched these elaborate dance costumes, didn't appear daunted. He requested her to bring her old dance costume along with a picture of the new variation. Then he accepted her request: all he did was look at it for a couple of minutes before setting out to sew the elaborate garment. The dancer was elated and soon, through word of mouth, my dad received more orders for *Bharatha Natyam* costumes.

My dad learnt how to sew men's suits and shirts in Kerala, but he was now stitching women's apparel, and it still amazes me how he managed to include these sophisticated classical dance costumes into his repertory. *Bharatha Natyam* was an Indian classical dance that originated in South India and was performed in temples, in the past, as an expression of love and devotion to the gods. Traditionally, the dancers were mostly women, but in modern times, the participants came to include men. The dance costumes were usually made from rich mulberry silk textiles in bright yellow, red, magenta, fuchsias, and peacock blues with borders woven in rich gold threads. The costume came in three parts: the blouse with sleeves was cropped at the midriff, followed by the pajama pants with pleats that spread out like a fan from the waistline to the knee. The fan-shaped pleats were meticulously stitched and ironed to stay in place. And there was a third modesty piece that was worn over the pants to cover just the buttocks of the dancer. The pajama pants were loose at the hips and tapered towards the ankles to facilitate vigorous dance movements. The costume enhanced the beauty of the dancer, especially when she struck a pose with her knees flexed out to display the fan of pleats in all its glory. By the 1970s, my dad's client base included a number of renowned dancers as well as owners of local Indian dance companies, like Bhaskar's Academy of Arts.

One day, a regular customer who was one of the founders of the National Dance Company of Singapore, came with a request for my dad to sew dance costumes for the entire troupe of Indian dancers, in preparation for a dance performance in Russia. I remember our shophouse being overrun by a bevy of beautiful girls. Our little home rocked with their laughter and chatter as my mum took their measurements. But I was never required to help out in any way. I was relegated to schoolwork. My only responsibility was to hit the books. I was also not allowed to partake in their discussions of the best fit, design or colour combinations, as much as I would have loved to. I was then in my early teens, and mesmerized by these dancers who wore dark kohl eye make-up, chunky jewelry and vibrant Indian outfits that exploded with mouth-watering colours. A few days after the measurements were taken for each dancer, my dad would miraculously complete another masterpiece. He would then display the stunning costumes with pride at the entrance of the shop, as you would show off a piece of art for all to admire.

From *Bharatha Natyam* costumes, my dad also extended his expertise to *Kathak, Kuchipudi, Odissi, Manipuri* and *Mohini Attam*. These were dance forms from different states in India. The designs of all these dance costumes were dramatically different, but dad was able to wave his magic wand to produce stunning outfits for all these classical Indian dance performances.

Many of the dancers would then invite their entire family to their dance performances in local theatres and auditoriums. Some of these performances were grand events performed at the Victoria Theatre or National Theatre, and graced by Ministers who were guests of honour. Our family, including my dad, would enjoy the evening of classical dance accompanied by live music. My brother and I grew up learning to enjoy these cultural events. We also knew how to discriminate between good dancers and the average ones, and the whole family would critique the performance together. These performances led to the beginning of our cultural engagement in the arts. In years to come, we would, as a family, attend not just Indian classical dance performances but also Indian musical events performed by famous musicians and vocalists.

Inspired by the dancers, my mum sent me at the age of eight to Indian classical dance classes taught by one of our clients. Unfortunately, I didn't have the inclination or the interest to carry through my mother's pet project. I was not endowed with feminine grace. Instead, I loved the outdoors. I enjoyed sprinting, hopping and skipping. I also found it difficult to display the myriad emotions from love to despair which was a critical part of the *Bharatha Natyam* dance movement. But go to dance classes I did, until the dance tutor, unable to endure my total lack of grace, reported to my parents that they were wasting their money. My dad was relieved. My mum had little choice but to give up her dream of seeing me perform the *Bharatha Natyam* on stage. My dad always had fears that it would distract me from my studies, as he silently harboured other dreams for me.

I am convinced that my dad was a very talented man but I don't think he thought so. He had developed and built his tailoring skills and knowledge from scratch. I think he undervalued his own worth as a talented artisan, although he had a fan club of very satisfied clients. For him, a formal education was what was worth aspiring for, and particularly one in a professional field. He felt strongly that besides commanding respect, it was the only means to a better life. When I was in secondary two, my dad was adamant that I study the pure sciences: pure chemistry, pure physics, and additional mathematics. He wanted me to be a doctor. I loved the idea, though my head was half the time in different worlds. I read Lobsang Rampa's "The Third Eye" and became fascinated by astral travels of the soul. I was mesmerised by the thought of souls transmigrating while the body slept. I read Perry Mason and Agatha Christie novels and was embroiled in solving mysteries. I read D.H. Lawrence's essays on henpecked men, and Guy de Maupassant's tales of pregnant young girls who created monsters by binding their growing stomachs to conceal their shame and fear of being chastised by society. I also read enough Mills and Boons romances, where handsome doctors, chiseled and sizzling, swept nurses or patients' daughters off their feet.

My dad's dream of me becoming a doctor sadly came to an end when we had three medical students reside with us for over a year. The students rented one room on the second floor of our shophouse.

All of them—Muthu, Ah Meng and Raman—looked miserable and ill most of the time. All three dragged their feet and had huge pimples the size of boils threatening to erupt all over their faces. They hardly laughed or joked, even amongst themselves, and displayed very little curiosity or interest in us, though they wanted their room cleaned a couple of times a week. On one of the cleaning days, I went up to their room with my mum, on the pretext of helping her. I discovered skeletons and skulls in an open chest amidst the mess they had left behind, which included half-eaten food decaying on their desks. I couldn't be sure if the skeletons were real, but I squirmed at the sight of them. I was also sure that somewhere in the rubble I would find dissected rats, guinea pigs and cockroaches. I avoided biology for that very reason. I couldn't imagine touching these dead specimens, even with tweezers. I was thus very happy to abandon my dad's dream for me, without his knowledge.

It puzzled me that as talented and interested as my dad was in his own craft, he never once encouraged me to learn dressmaking. I had absolutely no idea how those raw measurements got translated onto the fabric. Neither did I know how to use a sewing machine though I had seen, a million times, the feet on the pedal, turning the wheels that set the needle and thread in motion to sew pieces of fabric together. I had no idea. He would chase me away from the shop whenever I tried to mimic him cutting fabric. He did not want another tailor in the family, and that was final, regardless of whether I had the talent or the inclination. Even though the many challenges to his craft, over the years, brought a twinkle to his eyes and made him feel fully alive, I don't think he ever thought of his achievements as extraordinary. He remained unassuming but content.

Though my father's business grew, we remained in the small shophouse in Kampong Bahru. There were offers from *saree* shop owners to set up his business in their premises but my dad would flatly refuse. Until the end he remained a modest entrepreneur, and most importantly, as he wished, his own boss. He would neither consider expanding his business nor hiring other tailors to work for him. He led a relatively stress-free life as he managed enough work on his own terms. He derived a sense of fulfilment from ensuring that every piece of work was done to perfection. Upon retirement when he came to live with us, he would oblige some of his old clients. We brought his Singer sewing machine over to City Towers where my dad would spend some time sewing *choli* blouses and dance costumes for selected clients.

Remembering how truly content and fulfilled he was in his work made me rethink his retirement days. I was perhaps mistaken in my belief that dad was fighting to be relevant after he retired. In hindsight, I am more inclined to believe now that he may have been happy to play a quieter role as he watched us grow as parents. Besides, the pride and joy of being surrounded by grandchildren would have been immeasurable. He probably enjoyed his long leisurely walks in the neighbourhood and his weekly jaunts to the market, too. He just knew when to let go.

Chapter 9
THE SANCTUARY

AS HIS BUSINESS GREW in Kampong Bahru, in the backdrop of a neighbourhood buzzing with activity, my dad had opened his door to everyone. His generosity was overwhelming, and there were times when I questioned his trust and faith in people. Not everyone reciprocated his kindness, and some betrayed him. But it never stopped him. His kindness was spontaneous. I realized that he was not prone to overthinking when people were in need. I, for one, took his humanity for granted. I still wonder, *How did you make room for everyone?*

The king-sized bed that slept my mum, my brother and me was big enough to also sleep my mum's eldest sister, Letha. In 1961, having suffered a rocky marriage for many years, my aunt had decided to leave her husband in Malaysia and come live with us. I was five and my brother was one. My dad welcomed her. She was treated as family and she provided my mum with what proved to be great companionship. She would join us for all the family outings, and treated us as her own children as she had none of her own. The sisters gained confidence in the company of each other. Their conversations centred around the latest fashion designs in *sarees*, *cholis* and Punjabi suits, from the Hindi and Tamil movies they watched at the cinema every week.

My dad fueled their dreams by stitching all that their hearts desired. Before long, they were able to produce and parade around in breathtaking *sarees*, *cholis* and Punjabi suits embellished with their own embroidery, cross stitch, beadwork and mirror work. Both sisters loved to dress and added colour and vibrancy to their lives and our neighbourhood. They became trendsetters. It was not a marketing move on the part of the sisters to advertise their handiwork to make money, it was just pure vanity. And they were having lots of fun. To their amazement, it created a demand for the design of the clothes they wore. It also helped that both sisters were poised and well-spoken. Orders began to stream in from my dad's female clients who became their friends in the long run. Both sisters felt a surge of pride in their accomplishments. They would also do girly things like polish each other's fingernails, try different hairstyles, and groom themselves like the heroines in the movies. They posed for loads of pictures in their new outfits, sewn by my dad and enhanced with their colourful handwork. It was a celebration of their femininity and womanhood.

In all these instances, my dad was the willing photographer, always beaming with pride. Under my dad's roof and his watchful eye, my aunt started to sing again, as she gradually forgot the dark days of her married life. My aunt would write down the song lyrics from the movies and sing them while playing the *bulbultara*, a musical instrument with a simple keyboard. Instead of tears, there was now music and joy in her heart. She soon got a job at the Singapore General Hospital as a hospital attendant. She helped file case sheets because she knew how to read and write in English. My mum, who cried buckets when Letha first appeared at our doorstep, gaunt and withered, was elated at her transformation. My aunt was independent and free, and my mum loved her for it.

But soon her joy was interrupted. Her husband came looking for his estranged wife one day, and decided that he, too, would stay with us in Kampong Bahru. My parents cordoned off part of the living room to create some private space for the couple. Her husband, we discovered, was a polished gentlemen until he gave in to one too many alcoholic beverages. Even then, his verbal abuses were often hurled only at my aunt. My dad proved to be very patient with this man, who would listen to my dad's counsel respectfully, but lash out he would, unable to accept who his wife had become. But my aunt was no longer blindly abiding. She was a confident woman now, able to stand up to her husband and support him. My dad did what he could to keep the peace within the family until they found their own accommodation.

My Uncle Chith, my mum's older brother, was a regular visitor as well. He would visit us frequently as a young man whenever his ship docked in Singapore. He was the first person in the family to study in the United Kingdom. He received a scholarship from the Royal Malaysian Navy to study at Dartmouth College. He brought us many books, and stories and pictures of life at Dartmouth College. His stories were mostly of proms, balls and the beautiful girls he loved from his college days, and some from his travels as a naval officer. On one of his visits home, he surprised us with his Swedish girlfriend. She was the most beautiful creature I had ever laid eyes on. She wore a dark bob, had porcelain skin and dark attractive eyes. She brought us parcels of what I feel were dreams of lands beyond my imagination: little porcelain figurines and candle stands, and musical boxes that opened up to display a twirling ballerina that danced on tippy-toes to the tune of "Fur Elise." This was my first introduction to the western world, and this exposure shaped some of my aspirations to travel to distant lands.

Years later, after Uncle Chith left the Royal Malaysian Navy and joined the Port of Singapore Authority as a Deputy Port Master, he would drop by our shophouse for lunch, cooked by my mum, and a thirty-minute nap. This went on every day for many years. He slept undisturbed by all the sounds that surrounded that bed, the sounds of people moving in and out, sounds of the sewing machine, and sounds of the traffic along Kampong Bahru that was getting heavier by the day. Our home provided him with the emotional comfort and warmth that he needed then. He was divorced and had left his two boys in the custody of his wife who lived in Malaysia. My mum and dad did not question him about the breakup, nor was there any judgment. It was what it was. They opened their hearts to a lonely soul.

In my mum's and dad's home, there was always room for one more. One day, a seventy-five-year-old robust man whom we came to call *Thatha*, or grandfather in Tamil, came through the front door of our shophouse unexpectedly. He had taut skin that was so dark it almost gleamed with midnight blue light. His eyes were soft, warm and creamy with age. Thatha had worked for my maternal granddad in Butterworth. He said he had decided to leave Malaysia and look for work in Singapore as he had heard that the prospects for employment were better. He had also heard that Kuttan's second daughter was married and living in Singapore. So he came looking for my mum. He was a stranger, but my dad did not turn him away. He gave him a place to sleep under the staircase with a little shelf for his clothes. While he lived with us, he was entrusted to take me to school every day. It was a twenty-minute walk. He would carry my rectangular hard-cased brown schoolbag with one hand and take my little hand with the other, and ever so gently walk me to school. He would take the utmost care to navigate the narrow roads plied by huge trucks, wobbly and bursting with sand and gravel, as they came dangerously close to the pedestrians. The roads were being widened in the Bukit Merah area to facilitate better transportation for commuters as new schools emerged to accommodate a growing population. Silat Road at that time was flanked by monsoon drains and it was not uncommon for pedestrians to fall into them as they tried to avoid these merciless trucks on their mission. Thatha became a part of my school-going routine for a good year until he found a job as a security guard in a Japanese company. Once he began earning a modest salary, he would bring us sweets, fruit, pencils and erasers that he would buy on his way home from work. He would never fail to bring us little gifts every day. His eyes twinkled whenever he had something for us.

Just as with my dad, my communication with Thatha was silent, too! I don't recall having actual conversations. We exchanged smiles in gratitude. Three years later, I remember Thatha looking alone and dejected as he lay on a steel bed in a home for the aged in Nee Soon, in a ward with other inmates. The whites of his eyes were yellow with blotches of spidery red veins, ready to tear. His eyes turned inwards as we approached him, perhaps in shame, feeling abandoned, or perhaps in resignation. His silence was disturbing. I can't remember what we did or said to break the tepid air that hung heavily over us during that visit. I, for one, did not understand my dad's decision to send this dignified, trustworthy and dependable man to the home for the aged. Was it necessary? He had fallen and was bedridden. I told my dad we could take care of him. My dad simply said, softly under his breath, that it was not possible. He needed more medical attention than we could possibly provide, but dad promised we would visit him regularly. We did for a few months until we heard, one day, that he had passed on. My dad was moved just as we were, but he never dwelled on his emotions. There was a growing family to feed, school and clothe.

As I write this, as a mother of two children, it's beginning to dawn on me that in spite of the perceived lack of communication between my dad and me, the importance to him of providing care and support for those in need made an everlasting impression on all our lives. My dad left his footprints for us, unknown even to himself.

When I was twelve, my brother, who was eight, brought home a classmate who lived in overcrowded circumstances in a shophouse in Tanjong Pagar. He lived with his father and a million other tenants who led single lives, away from their families and children. My brother felt sorry for the boy who had to go home every day to a bachelor's den without a mother to greet him, cook for him or wash and iron his clothes. Neither did he have siblings to banter with or have a quarrel. This little boy, in spite of the squalid conditions, always looked clean and well-groomed with his short hair swept back neatly with Brylcreem. He became a friend of the family and was a regular visitor at our home in Kampong Bahru for many years. He would eat with us, chat with us and just enjoy the warmth of a home. He and my brother became bosom buddies throughout their primary school days. On the day of the release of the Primary School

Leaving Examinations results, my brother went to the Muniandy Temple in Silat Road to make a special prayer for himself and his friend. Both these boys topped their school in the Primary School Leaving Examination, and made it to Raffles Institution.

Their friendship continued through secondary school. We acted like his unofficial guardians because his father was at sea, literally, for long stretches at a time. After his "O" level examinations, he expressed interest in going to the Singapore Polytechnic but couldn't afford the fees. A loan from my mum helped the young man fulfil his dreams. Like his father, this boy grew up to be a seafarer. He wrote us letters of his life at sea and his various adventures, just as if we were his family. He would visit us without fail whenever his ship docked in Singapore. Many years later, we discovered that he had taken up recreational boxing and suffered injuries that caused damage to his brain. We heard that he had sought medical treatment in India and then we lost touch with him completely until one fateful day, we heard of his sudden death.

We were devastated. My brother in particular was saddened by this strange twist of fate. Because of the life they shared together as young boys, he felt compelled to observe a mourning period of sixteen days after which he arranged for the *atma shanti Pooja* (prayers for the peaceful passage of the soul) to be performed at the Shivan temple in the presence of family and friends.

Like my dad, my brother had a charitable heart. He was always happiest when he was able to give, and give generously he did of his money and his services. He tried to help everyone in need which, at times, was difficult to accomplish without making compromises. His staff, whom he took good care of, would joke about some of his free consultations. In 2017, he was awarded the Pro Bono Ambassador distinction by the Law Society of Singapore. The family did not get to know about his award and appointment until much later, through a friend. Like our dad, my brother was not one to give and gloat.

By this time, my dad was no longer with us. But he had left behind his legacy. There was always room for one more soul in our lives.

Chapter 10
OPENNESS. DIVERSITY. INCLUSIVITY. PEACE.

AFTER MY DAD PASSED on, I thought a lot about how a fifteen-year-old boy from a small homogeneous village in Chirayankil adapted and assimilated into Singapore which must have been shockingly diverse to him. How did he come to be so fearless and open to differences? How did he come to embrace diversity? He seems to have been comfortable with the idea of oneness, and grasped that we are more alike than unlike in spite of our different religious, social and ethnic backgrounds. His choices in life, I realised, reflected his openness. He had the audacity to start his business in a neighbourhood that was multi-religious, multi-ethnic and multi-lingual. It was not a predominantly Indian enclave. There were mostly Chinese, Indian Muslims and Malays in Kampong Bahru then. It was a bold move, especially considering that he spoke only his mother tongue, Malayalam, when he landed in Singapore. In order to assimilate into the environment, he learnt Malay without hesitation to communicate from day to day with not only the Malays and Chinese but the Indians, too, who did not speak Malayalam, but Punjabi, Telegu or Hindi. It enabled him to assimilate quickly into the local culture and be one with the neighbours. How did he come to be so comfortable with people who did not look, speak or dress like him? He did not allow unfounded fears to ruin his connection with people he encountered in his daily interactions. He wanted to be included and respected in this country, and was prepared to do the needful. He made assimilation his priority—to build friendships and connections that proved to be mutually supportive. Hence, his decision to send his children to mainstream schools, not vernacular schools, to get us integrated into the local community.

I think one of the major influencers in my dad's life, one that gave him the confidence and faith to do what was right regardless of race, language or religion, goes back to his adolescent days in Travancore. My dad was an ardent follower of Sree Narayana Guru whose creed, "One Caste. One Religion. One God. Is Man," resonated with him. This creed was a plea for mankind to embrace and respond to our common humanity. The Guru hailed from an area close to where my dad was raised in Chirayankil. I discovered from one of my conversations with my mum that dad was fed his first solid food by this lean and austere-looking guru. His parents plied a river on a small wooden boat, with a four-month-old infant in arms, to reach the guru's home for this auspicious occasion.

Sree Narayana Guru was a social reformer from an Ezhava caste in Kerala, as was my father. According to dad, the Ezhavas once held respectable vocations as ayurvedic physicians, warriors, martial arts trainers, traders, weavers and experts in astrology and spirituality. But they were displaced by the arrival of the Namboothiri Brahmins who belonged to a higher caste. With their arrival in Kerala, the Ezhavas were apparently relegated to menial jobs in the production of palm wine, *arack* and toddy (a variety of booze, I believe to keep the masses inebriated), although some Ezhavas did remain rich and continued in their trade of choice. In the days of the guru, only Brahmins were allowed to study Sanskrit, the language of Hindu Scripture. This meant that only Brahmins could become priests, because they alone could read and chant the Sanskrit mantras.

Driven by a deep sense of injustice, Sree Narayana Guru played a vital role in spearheading the democratization of some of the Hindu religious practices at that time. He fought established practices that discriminated against the underclass. In his teachings, he emphasized the common humanity of Man, rather than the rituals and traditions of the day which had been designed to give Brahmins alone the power to interpret and dictate scripture. In response to the elitism practiced in those days, the Guru built a Sanskrit school. He educated poor boys and orphans to lead a spiritual life of service, regardless of their caste, and gave the underprivileged children and adults opportunities to seek vocations that had been lost in the historical and political struggle. He proved that one no longer needed to be a Brahmin to be a priest; you needed instead to study and understand the Hindu scriptures, meditate, and lead a life of service to others. The Guru demonstrated through his actions that performing rituals and chanting mantras alone maketh a saint not. For his steadfast work, Sree Narayana Guru soon came to be revered as a spiritual teacher or *assan*, especially among young Ezhava men like my dad who must have felt empowered by his teachings and life experiences.

Discussions with my mother evoked stories my dad told us as children. One that I remembered vividly is of the Guru in his village. The Guru, we learnt, was a feisty character who was determined as a young man to follow his calling to be an ascetic. He studied Hindu scriptures in Sanskrit, meditated and reached a state of spiritual enlightenment, much to the chagrin of Brahmin priests who questioned the purity of his soul and his devotion to God. In a head-to-head encounter with a Brahmin priest, in the heat of the moment, Narayana Guru apparently challenged the Brahmin priest to throw up his food. "What you vomit," he said, "would be meat." The Brahmin priest scoffed at his adversary and accepted the challenge. When he threw up his food, lo and behold, the stench of rotten meat filled the air. Narayana Guru, in his anger, had used his spiritual powers to get this genuinely pure self-righteous vegetarian to throw up non-vegetarian food that he would never have actually consumed in his life. My dad used to get a thrill every time he related this story. But he was also quick to remind us that the Guru was deeply remorseful for having given in to his rage. He repented for many days thereafter by isolating himself in deep meditation and prayer.

The Guru attained *samadhi* many years later, in 1928. Once he felt that he had accomplished his dream of a more inclusive society, he willed his own death: he sat cross-legged in a cave, in meditation, until his soul left his body. By this time, he had made a strong impact in the minds of people, especially in the Ezhava community. I knew that what my dad admired most about Sree Narayana Guru was his courage to push the boundaries to create a new world order. We all understood where my dad got his spunky attitude. He was not one to slavishly accept his lot in life. He didn't believe in destiny, astrology or superstition. He believed in utilising one's *thandedum* (capabilities) to shape and fashion one's life.

In my childhood days, my dad would take us to Sree Narayana Mission which was established mostly by migrant workers from Kerala who worked at the British Naval Base in Sembawang. The Mission came to represent the teachings of the guru that emphasised humanity, and the importance of fair treatment of all human beings regardless of racial, religious or social differences. The Mission originated when it began raising funds for the needy by organising an annual "flag day." The funds were then used to offer educational bursaries to children from all races and religious groups.

Every year, for many years, my dad offered his shophouse in Kampong Bahru to be used as one of the many distribution centres on flag day. The empty tins would arrive at five in the morning, carrying the picture of the guru and his creed: One Caste, One Religion, One God, is Man. The call to acknowledge our common humanity resonated with many people in multi-racial and multi-religious Singapore. Most of the volunteers were students, like myself and my brother, and some adults, most of whom lived in the south of the island. They would gather at our shophouse to collect the empty tins and little paper flags. Then, we would hit the streets at around six, before daybreak, to catch port and railway workers and hospital staff on their way to work. Because it was a Saturday, we would find most of the people in a good mood. They only needed to put in half a day's work on Saturdays. Most of them would stop to give us their loose change of ten or twenty cents, while others would give us a dollar or two. Some would even engage us in conversation. They would want to know how the money would benefit others, and who it would assist. At the end of the day, the volunteers would drop off their tins, heavy with coins, at my dad's shophouse. The serial number on each tin would then be checked off against the name of the volunteer who used it. It would be sealed and handed over to the organisors. After which, the donations would be counted at the Mission. On flag day, I remember how my dad would do the family marketing early in the morning, and my mum would prepare a generous lunch and tea for the volunteers at our home. All day, my dad continued to pedal away at his sewing machine, greeting everyone and chatting with the volunteers as they walked in and out of our shophouse. This was the highlight of our lives for many years.

About a month after flag day, we would celebrate the Guru's birthday at the Sree Narayana Mission which was in Woodlands for many years before relocating to Sembawang. It was a big event for us. In the wee hours of the morning, the entire family would be involved in cooking *pachadi*, a yoghurt and water gourd dish, for at least a hundred people. We would then catch a taxi from Kampong Bahru, where we lived, to the Mission in Woodlands, to deliver the dish in time for lunch. The celebration was called *Chathayam*, named after the astrological star in which the guru was born. It was a potluck event where a number of families would each contribute a dish for the celebration, at their own expense. They would bring vegetarian dishes such as *sambar*, yellow *dhal*, *pachadi*, *inji pulli*, *thoran* and *prathaman*, which contributed to a day of feasting and camaraderie.

But it was also a day to acknowledge the hard work of the volunteers, and the sponsors for their support. On this day, we would, with bated breath, look out for the top collectors of flag day. My mum's older sister, aunty Letha, would invariably run away with the trophy every year. Then came the presentation of educational bursaries. Every year, my brother and I observed Chinese, Malay,

Indian, Eurasian—Christian, Buddhist, Muslim, Hindu—students walk up proudly to receive their cheques from the Mission. The donation provided financial assistance to students who needed support to further their studies. These simple gestures brought so much happiness to my mum and dad.

Today, Sree Narayana Mission plays a much bigger role in community care. While continuing to offer financial and educational assistance, the Mission runs Senior Care Centres and a Nursing Home for the elderly sick from which my family benefited, as life members, when my dad was terminally ill. Besides these services, the Sree Narayana Mission manages the Meranti Home that provides services and shelter for mostly psychiatric destitute males, many of whom were mentally burnt-out from the stresses of modern day work and life.

I realized where my dad got his ideas on diversity and inclusion. He raised us to be upright and, most of all, he showed us what it meant to be inclusive in a diverse community. These were subtle ways in which his values were imbued in us.

I also came to understand why my dad did not seem to be particularly religious as a young man. He saw religious rituals as superfluous engagements that could distract one from a humanitarian existence. For a very long time, as I was growing up, we did not have an altar for prayer at home. I was almost eleven when my dad was persuaded by my mum to erect a little altar at home. My mum was religiously inclined, as was her father who wrote poetry and prayers to music, in praise of Lord Krishna. These were the prayers my mum would chant every day. And so, my dad obliged. We had a number of deities in our altar in the bedroom, each to represent one virtue, but Lord Ganesha took centre stage. He represented the wisdom to know, and to make the right decisions. It earned him the title, *Remover of All Obstacles.* My mum would light the oil lamp every day, but I never once saw my dad pray at the altar.

There was no compulsion for my brother and me to pray at the altar, either. We prayed only when there was a pressing need—mostly occasions just before, during or after our examinations, and especially on the day the results were announced. My dad probably knew what my brother and I prayed for. Amused, he would keep reminding us that God helped only those who helped themselves. He didn't believe in freebies, even from God. If you wanted something you had to work for it, and not just pray for it. There were no shortcuts. We therefore did not grow up paying obligatory visits to the temple. Dad was also generally suspicious of religious institutions and organisations. He was skeptical of people who ran many of these religious groups. He felt that they tended to serve their own interests and egos. As an adult, I shared similar sentiments and stayed away from religious organisations. I, too, felt that it somehow tended to complicate the pure connection one could have with divinity. So unlike many of our Hindu friends and relatives, we were not members of any religious organizations as I was growing up. Our focus was always on service to those in need, and hard work to develop one's divine self.

In the last ten years of my dad's life, however, when he was in his seventies, there was a transition. Dad would pray every morning and evening for ten minutes, in his own silent way, at our altar at home. He did not chant mantras, recite Sanskrit scriptures or sing hymns in praise of God. He did not go through many of these customary Hindu practices. He did not observe fasting days or days of obeisance. He meditated, I realized, in his own unique way. There were no special techniques that he followed, but he achieved mental clarity, and inner calm and peace that was reflected in his positive outlook of life and unshaken faith. He was never bitter, even when things did not go the way he expected. For him, there was always light at the end of the tunnel. Every Friday morning at six, come rain or shine, he was there at Layan Sithi Vinayagar Temple in Keong Saik Road, and Mariamman Temple in South Bridge Road, doing special *archanas,* or prayers, for the entire family. He would, afterward, break coconuts. The shattering of coconuts in Hinduism symbolizes the surrendering of one's ego to the universe; it is an acknowledgment of one's mortality.

Over the years, as dad aged, the days and hours became quieter. There were no client orders to meet, no financial obligations to fulfill, and there were increasingly fewer responsibilities and duties to attend to. One seeks twilight—the spaces between blazing light and pitch darkness. In those hidden spaces, dad discovered a sanctuary within himself, and beauty that peace and stillness offers. Hence, like a pilgrim he sought his inner peace early on Friday mornings in Hindu temples, before workingmen, women and students appeared waiting to unleash their worries, anxieties and burdens onto Lord Ganesha, the remover of obstacles. My father learnt to appreciate those twilight moments away from a growing and bustling home frenetic with activity.

Remembering the Hindu rituals at the funeral, I wondered how my dad would have felt about it. I have little doubt in my mind, now, that he would have loved his own funeral. It was attended by many of the neighbourhood friends and relatives that he had lost touch with. I believe he must have felt their deep respect and love. Though I was not particularly religious at that point in my life, I gave in wholeheartedly to the rituals. It helped all of us express our love, care and concern for our father in immeasurable ways. The memory of the funeral for me was uplifting as it was colorful, fragrant and full of life. My dad would have loved it, for sure.

Chapter 11
WHERE ARE OUR ROOTS?

WITH THE PASSING OF time, many of the questions I had about my dad seemed to slowly unravel, gradually, like a spindle wound tightly with thread, helping to piece together a kaleidoscope of many-textured fabrics. I felt a rich tapestry coming into its own as the days went by. While some questions were answered, most evoked many more questions, and memories, too, that had been deeply embedded in the folds of my mind. My dad, in his twilight years, continued to be sentimental about his fatherland, in spite of having lived in Singapore for more than half a century. He always felt the pulse of India, and in particular Kerala, from the Malayalam newspapers and magazines he read, and from his friends and relatives who visited us from time to time. These visits were always special moments that brought a sparkle to dad's eyes.

I had to speak to my dad in my mother tongue, which was Malayalam, but being married to a Punjabi Singaporean, I spoke mainly English at home as my husband and I didn't know each other's mother tongue. He was Punjabi and I was Malayalee—a poor excuse, you may say, not to communicate in our mother tongue languages. So Malayalam soon lost its place in our household. Because my father was educated in Malayalam, my language loss resulted in fewer conversations between us. I did make some pathetic attempts to get my parents to speak to my children in Malayalam in their growing years. But it never happened. My mum, fluent in both Malayalam and English, chose to speak in English to my children. To this day, I wonder why they did not insist in communicating to my children in Malayalam. When I was a child, my mum would intentionally speak to me in English and ask me to translate her message to my dad in Malayalam. I was translating messages between my parents, from English to Malayalam and Malayalam to English, beginning at the age of three. It made my mum very proud to see my growing prowess at translation. If only she had persisted as a grandmother, I thought to myself, then my dad could have played a bigger role in my children's lives. However, it seemed impolite and crude to speak in a language that was alien to my husband. Or did they perhaps quietly decided to give in to a language that they deemed would reap far greater future benefits than their mother tongue?

I regretted that in our busy life raising a family in Singapore, we engaged my dad far less than we ought to have. Life was moving by so quickly that it was too much of an effort to even make simple conversation. I remember how my daughter once wrote a composition, in Primary school, of a granddad who spun magic threads, like a wizard, with his sewing machine. *I don't remember reading that composition to you, dad. I remember being moved by her affection for you, but in all likelihood, I let it slide. I should've read it to you. I should've translated it to you in Malayalam.* But the truth is, I didn't.

How did you feel about the slow erosion of your mother tongue, dad? The mother tongue connected you to your fatherland—the mother tongue was considered to be the language of the heart and the language of our dreams. The gradual erosion of the mother tongue was evident from one generation to another in our family. My daughter knew maybe three words of Malayalam: *Vellam venam*, meaning "I want water" and *Madhi,* meaning "It's enough." She had opted to study Mandarin in school, and so was effectively bilingual in Mandarin and English, though she spoke mostly English and probably dreamt in English, the language of our colonial masters. My son, on the other hand, was practically monolingual. He spoke only English. He would not even pretend to be interested in learning any other language, even though he studied Malay in school. Just as with my daughter, English would've been the language of his heart, the language of reason and the language of his dreams. As for my nephew, my brother's son, he spoke American and some Spanish because he left Singapore for the United States at the age of six. His only exposure to Malayalam would've been through my mum and dad. My youngest nephew, likewise, spoke English fluently and some Mandarin. While we were all equally culpable for the gradual erosion of our mother tongue language, I am still wondering what the main cause was. Was it the circumstances that dictated the mastery of English, at the expense of the mother tongue? Did we think we needed to be fluent in the English language to be successful? Did we perceive English as the language of the affluent? Were all of us, including my dad, subconsciously subscribing to these perceptions? Whatever the reason, we all became victims of convenience. We paid a price for it, because all of us could have had richer conversations with my dad and developed a deeper understanding of our heritage and identity.

Though my dad seemed to be attached to his home in Kerala, he did not consciously cultivate a love of the fatherland in us by making regular family visits to India. Being pragmatic, he probably got too busy earning a living and raising a family. Consequently, I hardly had any ties to the fatherland apart from knowing a few close relatives—grandparents, uncles, aunties and cousins—who lived all over India. At the age of forty-six, I had been to India but twice—once as an infant, and again at eighteen. What was my fatherland to me?

At eighteen, I received a Government of India Scholarship to read Physics at the Indian Institute of Technology in Kanpur in North India. Before I accepted the place in university, my family decided to send me to Chennai and Trivandrum to visit my relatives for a taste of its life and culture. My mum's family, in Chennai, was thrilled at the prospect of me studying in Kanpur. Being sentimental, they discounted the distance that stood in the way. Kanpur was about two thousand kilometres from Chennai. It wouldn't have been possible to make flying visits as they imagined. But my dad's younger brother, Renganathan, who was a poet and philosopher as much as a government of India senior officer, was considerably opposed to the idea. He was quite certain that a young Singaporean girl like me, many miles away from home, would not survive in such a terrain. I was convinced, too. During my stay in Trivandrum and Chennai, I couldn't walk the streets without being harassed. Men, young and old, would deliberately bump into me, grope or pinch me or rub themselves against me in crowded trains, bazaars and streets. Their actions were blatant. It puzzled me that they would grin, and not look away in shame. It was almost as if they felt triumphant. Though I found it revolting, I would not scream, shout or scare these obnoxious perpetrators. I would only glare and use my elbow to ward off their profoundly disturbing advances. Victimised, as such, I was happy to stay away from crowded streets and spend most of my time indoors with my mum's or dad's family. After this experience, there was no way I was going to leave Singapore for Kanpur. Fortunately, I had an ally in my uncle Renganathan who supported my decision, even using astrological charts that suggested that I would be lost and miserable in the jungle out there, if I ever decided to make the move to Kanpur.

So it was surprising that, thirty years later as a mother of a ten- and fourteen-year-old, I felt this sudden urge to introduce what I presumed to be my fatherland to my two children. Why did I do it? I had no idea. Was it for my dad? Where did this sudden desire spring from? Was it from the numerous Indian movies and songs that tended to romanticise life in India? Was it from the sentimental stories that dad had told us from time to time about village life? Was it about establishing one's ethnic identity—being Indian Singaporean rather than Singaporean Indian? Was it to draw from the well of our rich thousand-year-old heritage because Singapore was still budding as a nation? I had no answers.

But I did plan a holiday to my fatherland, much to the delight of my dad. My children were just as excited to get a taste of "Incredible

India", lured by television commercials that promised an exotic vacation. Having planned family road trips in Australia, I allowed my fingers to do the walking across the map of Tamil Nadu and Kerala, ignorant of the condition of roads, restaurants and sleeping places.

So began our journey to "Incredible India:" we landed in Chennai, spent a few days with my maternal grandma, hired a van with a driver with the help of a relative who volunteered to be our guide, and set off for Kodaikanal, a hill resort sought for its cool climate and green hills. The roads were bumpy and frenetic with auto-rickshaws, cars, motor bikes, cows, and women carrying their wares on their heads cushioned with rolled-up cotton scarves. Adding to the excitement, our driver was hell-bent on showing off his driving skills, weaving in and out of traffic that got us dangerously close to a pickle. But he got us to our destination in record time, in the midst of my daughter getting sick into a plastic bag throughout the journey, and all of us looking decidedly overwrought. Except my dad, who was springing with anticipation. The weather was cool and kind in the hills of Kodaikanal. It helped ease our nerves a little, but not for long. After a night's rest, we had to depart for Pazhani, in the hills. I wanted to take my children to the temple where I was fed my first solid food by a Hindu priest. We arrived at the foothills of the temple and checked into a guesthouse. The conditions were deplorable. My children refused to use the toilets, take a bath, or sleep on the sheets that were yellowed and musty. Most of all, they found the smells unique to small guesthouses to be strange and nauseating. It made us all feel queasy. But as adults, we felt we needed to be seen as accepting it with good grace.

Bracing ourselves after a short respite, we headed for Pazhani where Lord Murugan's holy shrine was located in the hills. We needed to walk up a flight of hundred meandering steps to get to the inner sanctum. There were now proper steps replacing the old dirt steps carved into the hill when I was an infant. The climb was easy, but with every step we were accosted by children, limbless and maimed, begging and pleading with their eyes, not so much for alms I felt, but for mercy, for pity, and for a way out of their wretched existence. A girl about my daughter's age and height, her eyes glossy with tears, looked into my daughter's eyes, silently pleading for the bottle of Coke she was sipping. My daughter handed it over without hesitation, hoping to perhaps awaken from the nightmare. She felt comforted when the girl smiled after taking a long sip. If only we could get rid of our guilt just as easily by simply giving them our loose change. Quietly watching the real-life drama was my son who, upon reaching the summit, broke down crying uncontrollably. It was too much for the ten-year-old to make sense of. Here we were, on our way up to meet a benevolent God, and there they were, children ten years old or even younger, ignored, abandoned and pleading for a little mercy. We were all equally shaken. How does one explain the extreme poverty, suffering and injustice? It was my children's first encounter with life, in all its splendour. I had no words, but I had to come up with an explanation without dismissing the suffering of those before us. When we reached the inner sanctum, there was only one question at the tips of our tongues: WHY? and only one silent prayer that seemed to be fitting: God save these souls, and lessen their suffering.

In the thirty-five years after I was fed my first morsel of solid food, this village had turned into a hive of organized crime—from child trafficking to racketeering of all kinds—to exploit visitors to the temple. My dad was so disillusioned. In anger, he kept chanting his mantra of life: *what prevents this country from progressing is the unconscionable cruelty or thushtatharam of man, so evident in people who don't care, in politicians who rape the land, and the rich who continue to turn a blind eye to the suffering of the needy. How can a country progress? That's why India is where it is now,* he kept repeating. He was somewhat ashamed, I think. He had seen this trip as an opportunity to show off his fatherland in all its glory to his grandchildren in 2002.

However, it would be remiss of me not to state that today, in our recent visits to India, the poverty is less apparent due to commendable efforts, not just by organisations but especially young individuals, to eradicate absolute poverty. There are even movements working genuinely towards providing food, clothing, shelter and free education to the needy.

After that 2002 soul-searching encounter, we were ready to leave the Pazhani hills to go to Periyar National Park and Wildlife Sanctuary near Thekkady. The brochures promised us tigers, lions and other wildlife, but all we sighted was an occasional elephant. We could live with the small disappointment, after what we had gone through in Pazhani.

After spending a night in Thekkady, we travelled for about six hours before finally arriving at my dad's village in Chirayankil. As we entered the house of his youngest married sister, we were amused to see a portrait of Stalin at the doorway, where Hindu families would normally have placed a picture or statue of a deity they worshipped. Kerala was governed by the Communist Party of India of Marxist-Leninist leanings for a good many years. My dad's brother-in-law was obviously a strong supporter, but I wasn't sure how the political affiliation would have translated into governance and socioeconomic equality because it was not very apparent to us then. Anyway, I was more interested in showing my children where *Muthacha*, or granddad, grew up as a young boy. We walked around his *krishi*, or agricultural land, which he had so generously given away. It was a tremendous moment for my dad when he told my children in Malayalam and a smattering of English: "This is where I grew up." They were excited to chase the chickens and goats around the *krishi*, but the cows wouldn't budge regardless how hard the children tried to unsettle these privileged creatures, worshipped for what they provided to sustain farming communities. We loved the fizzy sweet taste of fresh coconut water. We were told it was the best grade available. We couldn't stay at my dad's village, unfortunately, as there was not room for all of us. It was a fleeting visit that nevertheless created an everlasting impression for all of us.

After a one-and-a-half-hour drive, we checked into a hotel on Kovalam beach, a lovely beach skirted by coconut palms and sandy shores facing the Arabian Sea. My children were excited to see the ocean bursting and pushing its way dramatically onto the shore. The waves would have been excellent for surfing but, since none of us engaged in the sport, we decided to just wet our feet. We stepped into the cold water that was frothy and sandy with pebbles and broken seashells. The waves came roaring at us, mere mortals, on the beach. It was exhilarating until a six-story-high wave charged in from nowhere and knocked off the prescription glasses of my husband and daughter, leaving two helpless people blind on the beach, wondering what had just happened. I joked that it had happened to them because they didn't want to see the "real" India. Almost instantly, we were surrounded by fishermen and boys who promised to find us the two pairs of glasses. They were very convincing. For just two hundred rupees, they said they'd scour the beach and dive into the ocean! "Sir, you'll get your glasses by dusk," they promised in Malayalam. We parted with several hundred rupees, in vain, in hopes of recovering the glasses that were devoured by a giant wave.

After an eventful stay in Kovalam, it was time for us to leave. We stopped over briefly at *Kanya Kumari*, known as Cape Comorin during British colonial rule. Located at the southernmost tip of the Indian subcontinent, it was famous for its priceless views of sunset and sunrise. By now, we had been on the road for ten days and had covered a distance of more than a thousand kilometers. No one was in the right frame of mind to view anything. We were told by our guide and relative that on the way back to Chennai we had to stop over at the historic Madurai Meenatchi temple, built in the sixth century BC, in the 2,500-year-old city of Madurai. I explained that it is a historic temple, and at one time it was plundered by Muslim invaders, and rebuilt and restored. Look out for the *gopuram* which is typical of Dravidian architecture.

We arrived at the temple. It looked as if it had just emerged from the bowels of the earth, ancient and dusty, yet a survivor of the pillages of time. Its distinctive *gopuram,* or monumental tower, carved with several small statues, loomed into the sky and was visible for miles. The temple grounds, as we entered, were buzzing with tourists and locals. We received our *dharshan,* or blessings from a priest, without having to wait long. We found ways to get around the long queues at temples. But the jostle and hustle at the temple provided us with little spiritual space. My children got queasy once again, unfamiliar with the heady notes of incense, jasmine flowers and ghee lamps burning bright from hundreds of peace offerings to the goddess, Amman. Trying to get them to see the positive side of the experience, I continued, "This temple is among the many that celebrated feminine strength and power or *Shakti.*" My words, unfortunately, fell on tired ears too weak even to protest. We received our *dharshan* of *ladus* (Indian sweetmeat) to sweeten our lives, roses and jasmine to brighten our day with its fragrance, and *vibuthi,* or white ash made from burning the dung of cows, to remind us of our mortality. From dust we come and to dust we shall return. But now it was time to get back on the not-so-silky road.

On our way back to my grandma's home in Chennai, our relative and guide suggested once again that we stop over at a "very powerful temple." This time, my daughter developed a sudden headache and my son a stomachache. My dad told them to remain in the van. "*Tharakedila,*" he said gently in Malayalam with a knowing smile: "It's fine! You don't have to go. Just stay put." It must have reminded him of his many mandatory visits to the temple in his childhood days.

It took us about eight hours to reach our destination along roads similarly worn down with potholes that the driver avoided skillfully, along with the rest of the cars, motorbikes, cows and pedestrians on the street. We were relieved to have reached Chennai without running into any major trouble, save the runs and bouts of vomiting from time to time that interrupted our bumpy road trip.

In the cool comfort of my grandma's home, our relative, who took on the responsibility of being our guide this entire journey, suggested with much sincerity that we should go to the Sri Venkateshwara temple in Andhra Pradesh. It would be a four-hour drive from Chennai. It meant another eight hours or more on the road. Nobody was interested, not even my dad and mum. Our relative continued in all sincerity, "Most of the devotees who come to this temple are businessmen or those who are planning to start a business." We did not belong to either category. Businessmen would stick their business cards in crevices, cracks or gaps on the temple walls, hoping for good luck and blessings, and they would wait patiently for hours to receive their *dharshan* or blessings. People believed that besides one's *thandedum* or capabilities, luck played a critical role in business success. So they appeared at this temple, these businessmen and women, from far and wide. When my husband suggested that perhaps just he and I should go, his words were met with sighs of relief, even from my mum and dad.

The next morning together with our enthusiastic guide, my husband and I headed out at five to beat the traffic and the queues at the temple. Our journey was smooth, but when we got to the foothills we discovered that it was too late to receive our *dharshan* from the temple that day. We were told by the office that they had issued all the queue numbers for the day, and that we must take a queue number for the following day. I was ready to turn around and go back to Chennai, though we had already driven for an exhausting four hours. But our driver, a middle-aged Muslim gentleman, told us not to worry. Having done this route for many years, he knew some people who might be able to help. So after visiting a number of people he actually managed to get us a queue number for the same day. This Mohammedan gentlemen seemed very well acquainted with the temple premises and the proceedings. He guided us through the queues snaking their way for miles. He also seemed to know some of the priests. He told us to take our time with our prayers while he waited for us within the temple grounds. Here was Mohammed Kader, a stranger assisting us in receiving our *dharshan* at the Venkateshwara Temple at no extra cost. It was a moment to savour. The day was soft. There was kindness in the air. We sat on the clean, open grounds with the vast blue sky above us and felt the whisper of the gentle wind. That was a truly spiritual moment for us. We received our *dharshan* and met our driver who was chatting with some people he knew at the temple.

This road trip to South India had provided my young children with a lot more than they could process, but what was clear was that they were not at home in "their fatherland." Though our relatives lavished them with love and gifts, it was still not home. Singapore was home to them. It was familiar ground. To some extent, Singapore protected them and sheltered them from the harsh realities. Sadly, the initial euphoria and excitement they felt before the journey lasted less than a day. As we journeyed forth, it was replaced gradually with discomfort and dissatisfaction. They were still young, and we did not stay long enough in India for them to appreciate its rich cultural heritage and history.

When we got back to Singapore, I wondered if my dad was as happy as we were to be back in Singapore. After all, in India he was totally immersed in his mother tongue. I saw my dad come to life in India. He could once again hold forth and have his views heard. He was fully engaged with relatives and friends who spoke Malayalam. He would advise, congratulate and praise my younger cousins for doing well in their studies or work. He was animated when he spoke about our lives in Singapore. Though he seemed elated during our trip, it appeared that he, too, was happy to be back in Singapore. Home, it was. When the head hits the pillow in the safety of your own bed, all else melts away into oblivion. My father needed his daily routine, which included his long walks to the market, his trips to the temple, and the simple wholesome food that my mum cooked. For him it was a simple, peaceful life.

Chapter 12
UNDERSTANDING DAD

AS A PARENT, I came to realise that to understand dads and their role in a family, I needed to understand the culture of the times. Many dads, back in the day, were absent for months from their homes. With the advent of steamships, commercial travel became easily accessible, thus encouraging men to venture into unknown lands in search of lucrative jobs to support their families. Some of these absent dads worked in far-flung places. They would see their children perhaps once or, at the most, twice a year. Many of these children who never got to know their dads intimately were probably just grateful that they at least had dads who actually cared enough to feed, clothe and educate them by sending home money without fail. My dad, and many dads in those days, were driven by a deep sense of responsibility. They worked to live and to provide. They gave their whole lives to work. They were dependable men. Everyone understood this. My brother and I understood this, as children. Hence, our unquestioning faith. My mum understood this. She never once complained about the cooking, cleaning or the handwork she needed to do. She never once chided my dad for not baby-sitting, child-minding or teaching us. We carried with us a mental model of dads as providers of the family and disciplinarians whose primary role was to keep order in the household. We were, therefore, comfortable with the emotional distance. Dads were equally comfortable with the silence, and in some cases, physical distance. Their role was to provide. I don't think they wanted to do anything more. We never gave much thought to the lack of communication or intimacy.

I hardly ever laughed and joked with my dad. It was almost as if he needed to maintain his façade of propriety and authority so his children could grow up to be upright and responsible citizens. His conversations with us, as children, were largely about grades and even then, only if they were falling. He would lecture us, with his deep-set piercing eyes which used to send ripples of fear down my spine, but the pain and fear never did last long as I had a short memory for pain, and an even shorter memory for lectures. I was blessed that way as a child. I never harboured a grudge or dwelt on unsavoury moments.

When I failed my mid-term Mathematics examination in Primary 4, dad's whole being trembled with anger and he gave me a hard slap on my thigh. I cried and I was confused. I couldn't tell what went wrong in that examination. My father wasted no time. He had a friend who used to stop by his shop regularly, and dad hired him to tutor me. The young man, who was in his twenties, was a private tutor. After four sessions, this honest man who could've made more money from my dad, told him that there was nothing for him to teach me. He told my dad in Tamil, "Your daughter knows everything." I was just very careless and dreamy, as a child. I got bored easily, and the only thing that kept me interested was the life I experienced in the books I read, and the outdoor games I played with my friends in the neighbourhood. But poor grades were not an option with my dad. I had little choice but to focus and bring my grades up. Whenever my brother and I slipped up in our examinations, my dad would grind his teeth in anger and lament *"Vaashi venam."* It simply meant that we needed the grit and determination to succeed, which he thought that we sorely lacked.

There were, however, lighter moments when my dad would be in the mood for storytelling. When dad told his stories he would laugh, dramatise, slap his thighs in excitement and clap his hands. We could tell he was excited to relate the stories of events that took place in his village. I remember especially the story of the snake chases and how one day his great-grandma found a python in front of their house, struggling with a chicken bone that was stuck in its mouth. My great-grandma apparently pried open its mouth, pulled out the bone and let the python go. My father believed, according to village folklore, that no snake would ever harm any member of his family. We saved a snake and let it live! It was grateful! As a teenager, when my son was hounded by snakes chasing him around in his dream, I told him this story. In half jest, I told him he never has to be afraid of being bitten or attacked by a snake. He was, of course, skeptical and somewhat amused. We live in a logical world, so it didn't make sense to him. One other story that stuck was of a widow in dad's village who he believed was afflicted with a mental illness. She was not able to function normally; when she walked out of the house, she would imagine stones pouring from the sky like rain. It was so real to her that he said you could literally see her ducking the stones in trepidation of being hit. She couldn't eat in peace, either, because her food turned to worms and vomit whenever she beheld her food. My dad didn't believe, as most villages might have done in that era, that she must have been possessed by a spirit.

But most of the time, when he was in the mood for storytelling he would mostly make eye contact with my mum and occasionally glance at us, and be really happy that he had a captivated audience of his children. We would laugh along, but even then he would not let his guard down, relax and communicate with us directly. If we had questions we would ask my mum who would refer it to my dad. It was considered the respectful thing to do, I guess.

Not surprisingly, storytelling, banter and casual conversations tend to pay handsome dividends in one's twilight years. Stay-at-home mothers like my mum were ever-present for us; they listened to us, related their stories and played with us. Stories brought us closer especially when they were of personal childhood experiences. Once I became an adult, it was so much easier for me to communicate with my mum—to confide in her, to seek her counsel—and now as she grows deep into her golden years, I am able to advise her, to encourage her and to cajole her to do what is good for her. But for dads, who never really engaged with their children, the end can be lonely. It takes time to build friendly, communicative and reciprocal relationships, so by the time dads reach their silver years, it might be almost too late. Well-meaning and responsible dads of yesteryear lost out in a big way by playing a very small role in the lives of their children.

I realized that with western education, and exposure to the western media, my own mental model and expectations of a dad's and mum's role in the family had evolved. I questioned my relationship with my dad because I expected a friendly relationship, a shoulder to cry on, and a dad you can hug when you're down. Now I have become less judgmental and more willing to come to terms with my own dad, and with other dads of that era. In order to understand them you first need to understand the culture and expectations of the times. Their primary role was to provide. Many, like my dad, spent their entire lives playing out this role. Next, they saw themselves as disciplinarians in their children's lives. Hence the stern persona, lest their children stray and become hooligans and gangsters.

Today, a number of emancipated stay-home mothers expect their husbands to both toil away at work and carry on with their duties at home, all in the name of equal rights. These women would claim that they had been labouring equally at home: childminding, cooking, chauffeuring their children and carrying out the endless chores. They imagine that work in an office can't be as draining as housework. They feel the tedium of housework, the constant endless cleaning, and feeding children from one meal to the next. They contrast this to the workdays of their husbands, who have lunch breaks with colleagues and adult conversations about all and sundry.

In modern-day Singapore, however, we are quite lucky as it's easy to hire live-in helpers and part-time helpers to do the household chores that allow us to focus more on recreational activities and quality time with our families. Yet I know of cases where stay-home wives and mothers have actually fired their live-in helpers just so that their husbands would *not* kick off their shoes, slump in front of the telly, and wait to be served. These women want dads to be around to contribute to the household chores—do the dishes, laundry and the ironing—after a hard day at work. As a working wife and mother of thirty years, I know what a struggle it is to multi-task. I used to come home, completely depleted after a day at school, and just wanted to kick off my shoes, slump in front of the telly and wait to be served!

Like my father, I was a provider. I contributed to mortgage payments. I contributed to a lifestyle. I wanted my children to go to good schools to have a holistic education. There were music classes, art classes, tennis lessons, "mother tongue" lessons—I needed to contribute to their wellbeing and I needed that job. I needed that salary at the end of the month so I could share the financial burden with my husband. But what I did wasn't just a job. I am not a pen pusher or an administrator, crunching numbers. Instead, I work with children who have dreams and aspirations. I deal with families for many of whom education is the only means of not just survival but a better life.

Like the parents of many of the children I taught, my dad also made sacrifices to educate us. He recognized education as a social leveler that provided families and communities with opportunities for upward mobility. But for my dad, more importantly, he saw education as a means of liberating a person from the shackles of "dos" and "don'ts" dictated by those in power at any level. For my dad, education opened up choices and different platforms to exercise the interests and ambitions of an individual. It was not just about climbing the social ladder. I understand how my dad felt about education, and in many ways, I can see how I have been similarly influenced.

As a full-time working parent, I came home physically and emotionally exhausted from work. Teaching was not just a 7.30 to 3.30 job, as is commonly perceived. School hours were spent not just teaching. There were remedial lessons to help struggling students to meet the minimum standards, and relief duties for teachers absent from work. The rest of the time was spent chasing recalcitrant students for their assignments, or making house visits to haul reluctant ones back to school. There were also students who wanted counselling sessions that were more like a pair of ears and eyes to listen to their woes and see to their needs—the list of duties could go on indefinitely. It was a luxury for me, as a teacher, to be able to complete grading the scripts or preparing the tutorials and lectures in school. So, like most teachers, I lugged my laptop, piles of papers and exercise books home.

I understood how, at the end of the workday, one needed a respite. One gets annoyed and irritated when dads switch on the television the moment they get home, and then have their dinner sitting, looking at moving images, while their minds drift or continue to dwell on the goings-on at work. Some others find relief by meeting up with the boys to discuss politics and world affairs. To discuss anything really—to keep their minds off their responsibilities and duties. I understood the motivations behind those actions.

I realized how much I, too, have sacrificed by turning my attention to work during my children's formative years. How do you motivate your children? How do you teach your children? You are consumed. You are exhausted. You know what to do but you are impatient. You want quick fixes. Quick returns. Instant learning. Finish your homework. Why haven't you finished your homework? There's just so little time. There are swimming classes. Art classes. Music classes. Cricket. Squash. Roller blading. Cycling. There are only so many hours in a day to complete the mountains of worksheets piling up in the bedroom, spilling out of open bookshelves onto the floor, leaving a trail all the way to the dining table where the homework is done, because the desk in the room is not big enough. Worksheets after worksheets, and we're still not done. I have work tomorrow. There's marking, more papers to be corrected. I need to complete them tonight. I promised to return them tomorrow. The minutes speed by, the hours arrive too soon like unwelcome guests in the middle of the night.

We wanted our children to have a holistic education and not spend time at tuition agencies unless they had to. But what could you do when ninety percent of the students had private tutors, and parents who carted them from one tuition agency to another almost all day? Many of my children's peers in school were ahead of the syllabus by at least two years. My ideals for children to learn through discovery went right out of the window. I was caught out. At that juncture, I was not sure what to do. As a parent, you cannot afford to be conflicted. You have to do what you need to do—with conviction. We wanted our children to do well in examinations without having to make compromises.

We wanted them to learn how to learn, and learn how to "monitor and manage" their own learning, and most of all, to learn through discovery. Grades mattered to us, of course, but we also wanted our children to have fun and discover the joy of learning! But we were too tired after a day's work to fight the culture of testing, driven by high-stakes examinations, and we failed as parents to motivate, to engage, to cajole, to entice our children… there was just no energy.

Chapter 13
OUT OF THE SHADOW INTO THE LIGHT

IN 2015, ELEVEN YEARS after my dad passed on, he appeared in my dream. It was 5 a.m. He looked sad, startled. I woke up worrying that it was a sign that my mum was ill. I went to check on her, but she was curled up in bed like a baby. Relieved, I went back to bed. I fell asleep almost instantly. An hour later, in my dream I was weeping and my dad looked at me with his sad, piercing eyes and whispered almost inaudibly, "Why are you crying?" *"Neerashakal ondo?"* "Do you have any regrets?" I woke up, alarmed and distressed. The question kept repeating in my head for hours thereafter. It disturbed me. Why? Why now? I thought about my role as a daughter and a parent. I realised that I had a number of regrets. And, just as I had a number of misgivings as a parent, I wondered if my dad did, too, in his twilight years. I WhatsApped my brother after a couple of days of tossing and turning the dream in my head. I wrote him: "Perhaps the only regret I had was that I never really bothered to communicate with Acha while he was living with us…I didn't know how to…."

My brother's prompt reply came: "Shal, you just communicated with him, and remember that ninety percent of communication between people and especially connected souls is nonverbal. You looked after Acha like a truly filial daughter, so no regrets, please." It was comforting. I needed to move on.

That was a turning point for me, and I began to focus less on the perceived problems. I wrote, and as I continued to write and recollect, I remembered how my dad seemed to have provided so much with so little. I remembered all the angels in our lives and the gifts we may have taken for granted. I had been thinking of myself as having emerged from poor circumstances, but now I realise we were far from impoverished. My brother and I grew up with abundance, and an abundant mindset, because there was always more than enough of everything we needed. We never feared going hungry or not being able to pay our school fees or affording to buy books, cinema tickets or clothes that we liked. Were we poor? I wonder if statistically we would have been considered poor. We had a roof over our heads, though we did not own it. It was not a squeaky-clean sterile living space, but it was hygienic enough to prevent us from falling victim to life-threatening diseases. We had clean drinking water piped into our homes that was affordable. The rentals were low. I remember my dad paying an average rental of $35 to $50 monthly, for years, for a shophouse with four rooms and two spaces sufficient for a tailor shop and a barber shop. The property was at the heart of growing businesses. It was close to amenities: the hospital, coffee shops, markets, mission schools and neighbourhood schools and a post office. Because the hospital was ten minutes away, medical care was immediately available. There were no waiting lists for medical appointments, and medication was affordable because it was subsidised by the government.

Home was a haven. We had the luxury of having a stay-at-home mother. Our meals were home-cooked and healthy. At lunch, there was fresh meat and vegetables that my dad would have picked up from the wet market that morning. In true Kerala style, we grew up eating seafood. Kerala is in the southern tip of India, and is well known for its fish from the Indian Ocean and rivers. We had fish curry at least thrice a week, and crab and prawns once a fortnight. So, I learnt to eat fish called *mathi chala* with a million tiny bones. I was also adept, from a very young age, at deshelling prawns and crabs. We could afford a variety of vegetables from the market. We had water gourd, snake gourd, bitter gourd, turnips, tapioca, pumpkin and legumes. Our food was cooked with fresh spices like coriander, cumin, mustard seeds, cinnamon, cardamom, and dried and fresh chillies, roasted and ground at a mill in Serangoon Road. We used generous portions of garlic, shallots, onions and turmeric in our cooking. And for breakfast we had half-boiled eggs, milk and Milo. There was also a battle to get us to consume cod liver oil capsules, and sometimes the ghastly liquid version which was deemed to be better for our brains. My dad was draconian at the dinner table. He would lecture us on the vitamins in various foods. He would insist on us finishing our food, and especially the green vegetables and *dahl* that we so hated. There was a cane at the dinner table, just in case any of us decided to leave some food behind on the plate. My mum would add to the rhetoric by lecturing us on the starving millions, and how one teaspoon of egg yolk is a meal for a growing baby.

My stay-at-home mum was our first teacher of English and arithmetic. She taught us to read, count and do mental calculations. She didn't like us using our fingers to add or subtract. Together with my aunt, they would ensure that we spoke grammatically correct English. They also did not condone "Singlish." We weren't allowed to punctuate our sentences with "lahs" or "mehs." My brother and I had a head start in primary school because we were taught basic literacy and numeracy skills at home before attending school. In my early school days, my dad never appeared to worry about anything, most probably because he was quietly watching from behind his newspapers as we grew up. He would whistle happy tunes from Malayalam, Hindi and Tamil movies.

We celebrated special occasions. On our birthdays or special festivals like *Onam*, my mum would cook fifteen different vegetable dishes. On Diwali, we had all the meats from chicken, mutton, *Ikan kurau* to prawns, served with at least four or five different types of vegetable dishes. We had enough food to share with family and friends, some of whom lived with us for long periods, while others visited us regularly. There was always enough for everyone.

Though I went to a neighbourhood school, and our education was heavily subsidised by the state, my brother and I encountered some of the best teachers. Miss Tan SL, who was in charge of the Brownies and Guides, would organise day-long excursions, hikes and camps. I remember hiking up Mount Faber, and discovering a stream of crystal clean water from which I drank. She taught us life skills from how to start a fire for cooking in the woods to how to attend to injuries. She knew everything about me because she would talk to me, not just about school and homework, but about my family circumstances as well. If I grew moody, she would pick up on it and ask me if all was well. When I graduated from being a Brownie to a Girl Guide, she lent me her well-starched uniform so that my family wouldn't have to incur an extra expense. I didn't even have to ask—she just offered. My teachers and leaders seemed to be genuinely interested in us children, as people. Some would even invite us to their homes for a meal and surpervise our homework. I remember Miss Tao, a former nurse-turned-teacher who would invite us to her family flat located fifteen minutes from school. She would serve us soft drinks and cakes, and we would do our needlework while we listened to the cable radio service and her life stories. She would tell us ten-year-olds why she quit being a nurse, and what she loved about teaching. She was the first teacher to read my English composition, in class, aloud to the other students. She discussed the effectiveness of a metaphor I had used in my writing to describe an experience. The affirmation I received that day had far-reaching implications. That simple gesture created in me a sense of myself as a writer. I no longer wrote just for the teacher or to complete an assignment—I wrote to communicate and reach a wider audience. Miss Tan, my Primary 5 teacher had a library corner in her classroom. She would read us excerpts from the books from the library to entice us to borrow them. In her class, I completed reading the entire Enid Blyton series of books. Miss Tan also seemed to genuinely enjoy our company. She would take us to the cinema. Her class watched the "Sound of Music" and "Mary Poppins" with her. She would also invite us over whenever her family rented a holiday bungalow at Tanah Merah or Changi Beach. Before meeting her family, the class would get a lesson on the rules of etiquette and good manners. We would be reminded to greet everyone, and say "please," "thank you" and "goodbye." She was very proper that way. She would tell us that she wanted her family to think well of us. She didn't want her family to think of us as riff-raff from the slums of Bukit Merah.

My brother, who was somewhat mischievous, would have his teachers travel all the way to my dad's shop to complain about him if he was naughty. One day, Mr. Samy came huffing and puffing, having to lug so much of himself, into my dad's tailor shop. My dad got a blow-by-blow account of all the goings-on in school. He told my dad about how my little brother was mixing with bad company, and how his friends were disrespectful when told off that day for bringing a knife to school. There was no WhatsApp, but the information was relayed just as instantly, with gusto, to my dad—who would then spring to action. In the days of secret societies, it was every parent's nightmare that their son would become a gangster. Some of my brother's lady teachers were my dad's clients. They had a soft spot for my brother because he was bright and articulate, and they would give my dad a report on my brother's academic progress whenever they visited my dad's shop—unlike all the other parents, my dad didn't have to wait for his son's school reports.

Children like us from "neighbourhood" primary schools, or schools in locations which were not in prime districts, qualified for some of the best schools in the nation, including Raffles Girls School and Raffles Institution. We also had opportunities for university education. All the mischievous boys who taunted Mr. Samy did brilliantly in the Primary School Leaving Examination, and all qualified to attend Raffles Institution. One of the boys who my brother and I played marbles with in our back yard, is presently a district court judge, and another ended up as a member of parliament, while some others like me became teachers, head teachers and master teachers in schools.

As children, we were not bogged down by homework and worksheets. There was just enough homework for a teacher to check for understanding, and reinforce the learning done in the classroom. Apart from that, we were free to play and explore. There were treasure hunts that took us to railway tracks, wild bushes, expansive green fields and mossy orange green drains teeming with life. We played with tadpoles, baby spiders and grasshoppers, and let them go into the wild. There were friends, neighbours and parks waiting to be discovered—all in my backyard. I also had the luxury of being me. I was precocious as a child. I ran everywhere. I ran into a neighbour's metal gate; I ran into a pot of hot water, sizzling and ready to eat into my skin. I ended up with stitches and third-degree burns. In short, I always ran into trouble. There was blood, raw pink wounds stinging with pain. There were tears, bandages and lectures on being more careful, but I was never grounded. I learnt to pick myself up and carry on. All we needed to do was to produce the grades, and we were given the freedom to explore. My brother and I took full advantage of the situation. My dad seemed to carry with him a positive mental picture of children playing and enjoying their childhood, free from worry.

My dad's temperament suited us children. He was strict and he hardly chatted with us—but he let us be children, to run, to play, to be mischievous. And we knew he cared as we watched him pedal his Singer sewing machine to provide us with a solid foundation inspired by a simple wholesome life. Besides, when we compared our dad with that of our friends, we realized how fortunate we were. He did not impose all kinds of regimens on us. There were broad guidelines and expectations within which we had the freedom to explore and discover ourselves.

That was perhaps what contributed to my brother's personality. He turned out to be an independent free spirit, much to the dismay of my dad at times. He just loved projecting his bad-boy persona, which got him as many admirers as troubles back in the varsity days. He was bright and athletic, but notoriously playful. He had a photographic memory, a way with words like no one I know, and to top it all, he played water polo for the university and had a fabulous physique. In other words, he had all the ingredients for a potent brew. One day, one of the girls he got to know in varsity, told him that she was surprised that he didn't look like a tailor's son. Amused, he retorted, "Did you think tailors' children ran around with stitches on their faces?" It was funny!

Suresh, my brother, turned out to be a diligent and savvy lawyer. His mammoth memory, gift of the gab and charm that got him into all kinds of trouble in law school served him well in law practice. He is recognized for his work in civil, criminal and commercial litigation. Over the years, he has won several landmark cases that have become compulsory reading for local law students. Besides running his own law firm, he was also appointed a Referee of the Small Courts Tribunals by the State Courts of Singapore.

Like me, my brother has also had some inexplicable encounters since my dad passed on. On one of his visits to a client on death row, after an emotional exchange, the client held my brother's hand and whispered, "Sir, you don't have to ever worry. I can see someone by your side, right here. It's your dad, and he will always be there to guide you and protect you." My brother, of course, was skeptical until his client continued in a low voice, "Your father was a very good tailor, right, sir?" My brother froze as there was no way his client could have known this about him. Anyway, my brother chose to be comforted by the thought.

My brother's boutique law firm has a dash of all the things my dad stood for: honest hard work, compassion and fairness. His team of lawyers and staff live and work by this guiding principle: every single life matters. These lawyers are committed to providing the highest quality of legal service and care to all their paying and *pro bono* clients. As you enter my brother's office, you will see an enlarged portrait of my dad on the left wall of the cubicle. He believes, till this day, that my father is watching over all of us, and so do I.

1962 – Singapore – Picture taken in a Photo Studio in Tanjong Pagar. My brother, Suresh is 2 years of age and myself 6. My dress was sewn by Dad.

1960 – Singapore – Dad and I with aunty Letha, my mum's older sister, (left) and Mum (Indira) by her side. My dress, Mum's and Aunty Letha's Indian choli blouses sewn by dad while handbags knitted and crocheted by Mum and Aunty Letha.

Mid '60s – Singapore – Family portrait.

Mid '50s – Palghat, Kerala, India – My mum with Aunty Prema (mum's younger sister who became a well known actress in Kerala).

1950s – Singapore – My dad, seated second from left with his friends.

Mid 1950s – Chirayankil, Kerela – Family portrait of Dad's family in India. First visit from Singapore to Dad's village in Kerala after I was born in 1956. Dad (standing 4th from the left carrying me), Uncle Renganathan (Dad's younger brother standing second from left), my dad's mum (Seated third from the left) and my mum (seated fourth from left).

Late '50s – Singapore – Kampong Bahru shophouse. Dad with me lurking behind waiting to create mischief.

Late '50s – Singapore – Kampong Bahru Shophouse – Dad and I.

1960s – Singapore – Shop houses in Kampong Bahru.
(Courtesy of National Archives of Singapore)

Part 3

Light Lines

Every breath, deed or word
Silent, spoken or written
Inspires a light line.
It has a nose.
It sniffs and seeks
Companion light lines.
What a find,
When minds, hearts and souls meet
Creating rambunctious waves,
Gyrating in random movements
To the beat of different drums:
Tabla, wadaiko, bongo, tanggu, conga
Wild and ecstatic
Like fireworks
They explode in the night sky.

Chapter 14
REFASHIONING THE BLUEPRINT

IN HIS SIXTY-FIVE YEARS in Singapore, dad witnessed the miracle of Singapore, and the complexities it brought on with it as it developed into a city with almost first-world standards. By the time he retired, more than eighty-five percent of the population in Singapore was made up of "middle-class property owners" which was great, but it also meant a lifetime of mortgage payments for many of these property owners. If you add a car loan to the equation, you have a nightmare in your hands because prices of property and cars were exorbitant. Servicing hefty loans had implications on family life. It often meant that an average family, needed a dual income to sustain a family with one or two children. One could also use the monies accrued in Central Provident Fund (CPF) Savings, through employer and employee contributions, to service home loans. Many did. But the Government's Central Provident Fund Policy was initiated mostly to encourage working Singaporeans to save part of their salaries for retirement and old age. If most of one's savings in CPF are used to service home loans, what would remain for retirement and old age? Not much. In fact, unless the property values appreciate and you are able to sell your home for a profit, you would forever be worried about money for old age. Times were different. The challenges were different and complex. My dad watched how my husband and I managed our dual income in order to afford some of the simple things in life. Ironically, all we wanted was more physical space and psychological space. In land-scarce Singapore, it was a challenge. We wanted our children to have a childhood as we did. There had to be time—to play, build friendships, explore neighbourhoods, and make discoveries about people and the world around us.

My dad also observed the effects school life had on his grandchildren and his children. In less than half a century, school life had taken on a complexity he may have had difficulty understanding. The Ministry of Education took pride in how "every school (was) a good school" but private tuition had become a way of life by the '80s, at every socio-economic level. Private tuition was not just for the rich. Children from the middle and lower income families, too, were sent to private tuition centres after school, in the evenings and on weekends, starting in preschool and onwards. It was a multi-billion-dollar industry, with most parents spending a whopping part of their salaries to prepare their children for examinations in every subject. The rich, undeniably, had an edge, being able to afford the best tutors and enrichment programmes. This gradually had implications for teacher expectations and pedagogy in schools. Back during the days of my dad, most students went to school to be taught basic literacy and numeracy skills. Today, most primary school teachers expect their students to have acquired these basic skills even before they enter school, because it facilitates the swift completion of worksheets, assignments and tests that kickstart the beginning of a child's school life. My dad was cognizant of how our lives had become complicated and frenetic in pursuit of a better lifestyle. There was never enough physical space and head space.

What would my dad have said? For him, Lee Kuan Yew remained a saviour. My dad saw Singapore grow from a village to a city with impressive world-class infrastructure. The evidence of Lee Kuan Yew's leadership and vision was everywhere in Singapore by the 1980s; there were new roads, highways, pedestrian bridges, malls, schools, hospitals, mass rapid transport systems, and of course parks and trees that seemed to grow overnight. Singapore earned itself the reputation for being a Garden City; green, safe and squeaky clean.

Singapore was a financial hub, and the strong Singapore dollar made travel for work, leisure and study abroad more accessible than ever before. Lee Kuan Yew had put an end to secret society activities and the infamous racial riots that plagued the nation at one time. But Dad did not judge us. Societies evolve and so must we. Having gone through bread-and-butter issues in the 1960s, he saw these problems as typical of those that emerge as expectations change in a society becoming more and more affluent in some ways. Questioning and challenging issues, constructively, would be what he would expect of its people. It could lead to a way of life that we may not yet have conceived. But if all efforts to find a comfortable space fail, there is always the option of uprooting for greener pastures, like he did.

We wanted more out of life. The choices and decisions we made were certainly influenced by the foundations laid by our forefathers. It is what, perhaps, gave us the confidence to navigate uncharted territory. My husband and I applied for permanent residency in Australia. We were sure at that time that it was the way forward because it would buy us more space with the current assets we had acquired. But we were not willing to leave our jobs as yet. If we were to uproot, we'd be living on our meagre savings until we found jobs in Australia. A move also meant leaving our parents who were getting older. It was a tough decision on all counts. So, we decided that we would first send my twelve-year-old daughter to a boarding school in Melbourne until we were ready to make the big move. We did our research and, hand in hand, my daughter and I visited several private girls' schools to suss out their culture and academic standing. We also spoke to several friends and acquaintances who had already made Australia their home for the sake of their children's education. There was a long waiting list in some of the best private schools in Melbourne, as it was not uncommon for parents to put their children's names on the wait list at birth. And here we were, trying to gain admission into Methodist Ladies College, three months prior to the commencement of the school term. As fate would have it, my daughter's interview with the principal of Methodist Ladies College went well, and my daughter was given a place in both the day and boarding school on the spot. There happened to be a single vacancy in the one school that we both liked. What impressed us about the school was the energy and the warmth of the students. It was their break time, but the girls came running to help us, and they showed us the way to the principal's office during their break. Australia was also familiar to my children by that time because most of our family holidays were spent in various parts of that country. We enjoyed the open spaces and our interactions with nature that these countries afforded; the Blue Mountains, Grampians, farms, woods, rivers and lakes. The whole family, including my dad and mum, loved the long drives, the smell of eucalyptus trees in the woods, the sounds of surf breaking along the shoreline, *al fresco* dining in the summer months, and markets of fresh vegetables, seafood and meats.

How did my dad feel about sending our daughter away at such a young age? My dad appeared calm at our decision. He had always put a premium on education, and when we explained that it would be better suited to help her find her balance between work and play, he was convinced. My dad did not feel that she was too young and he was confident that she would manage. He was positive and supportive of the move. While I obsessed over the possible abuse of my daughter's early childhood freedom, my dad saw it for what it was. Boarding school would come with all its rules and regulations to keep the boarders in check. If anything, what he lamented was that the lack of freedom would stifle my child's free spirit. When he was a fifteen-year-old, living away from home, he did not squander his time and mishandle his freedom, so he did not expect his granddaughter would.

As parents, my husband and I grew with our children. We became more attentive, resilient and patient with every passing day. The journey was not easy by any means as there were tears and fears, including phone calls from my daughter pleading to come home when loneliness set in and she started missing home. There were many difficult conversations, but I would always try to get her to see the bright side of being educated away from home. We saw a change in her. After a month in school in Australia, she began to take charge of her own learning. There was no one to remind her of her daily chores and homework. She got to enjoy solving math problems, which she had once detested, and pushed herself to complete the more difficult exercises. It surprised us. She would also set the alarm, and get up at 5 a.m. to attend badminton practice at 6 before the start of school at 8.30, on cold winter mornings. In summer she was up at dawn, training for swimming competitions. Her learning was self-directed and she was growing to be an independent young lady with strong opinions. At twelve, she had to write an opinion piece on where, as a young girl, she would want to grow up: Sparta or Athens? She sought my opinion. I said Athens, because it was the seat of knowledge, arts and civilization. She disagreed with me and chose Sparta instead. I was disappointed until I heard her reasons. Of the two, she said young women in Sparta had more opportunities to receive an education, though it was limited to dance and sport, whereas in Athens women were not entitled to formal education of any kind. I checked the facts, and found there was some truth in it. But more importantly, I was pleased that she was growing up to value her own opinions, and appreciate the importance of equal rights for men and women. The written piece was also well argued as it was driven by strong personal beliefs that she was beginning to develop.

In the three years my daughter was in Melbourne, my husband and I made several separate trips there to ensure that she was settled and happy. She excelled in school, and applied herself diligently to both her studies and sport. But we learnt that she was waiting eagerly for us to make the big move to Australia. She saw herself as a pioneer of sorts, in this scheme. But once she realized that both her parents had lost their nerve and reneged on the promise to take up permanent residency in Australia, she was distraught. She did not want to stay in Australia any longer. She did not want to spend the rest of her adolescent years away from us. Her explanation was that this was the only time she would have with family until she reaches adulthood, and it made sense. We had sent her away when she was only twelve. She was too young, we realized, and now she was pleading to come back home to family unless we uprooted. So, it was back to Singapore for my daughter. Having been away from the local secondary school system, she was permitted by the Ministry of Education in Singapore to attend the United World College of South East Asia, a private school, in the Dover Road campus, in Singapore. We had to seek permission from the Ministry of Education, because it was mandatory for all Singaporeans to attend local government schools unless the circumstances were special.

Three years later, at the age of fifteen, our son, too, began attending a boy's boarding school in Auckland in pursuit of a holistic education. My son was endowed with exquisite hand-eye coordination and motor skills. He excelled in squash and cricket, and played at both school and national levels in Singapore. I also realized that he had a flair and interest for literature and history, but not the sciences which brought his average scores down. Besides, the science curriculum in school was way ahead of what was required for the "O" levels. The school was testing way above standards. Just as success breeds success, failure has a stultifying effect on one's motivation and morale. So, he put more of his time and energy into sport, encouraged by the results it bred. His science teachers were livid, and at every parent-teacher meeting they would advise us to get him to drop his sporting commitments. They would advise him to stop playing so he could focus on getting his grades up. With that meeting my son's fate was sealed. We knew he was talented, especially in squash, and should continue playing while developing his interest and flair in the humanities. We decided, that day, to send my son to school away from home. By now, my dad was no longer with us but I knew he would have approved. My son was fifteen, the same age as my dad when he left Kerala for Singapore—not to study, but to work and support an entire family.

My husband and I selected Auckland Grammar School as it was both strong in academics and squash. We hoped for him to find a balance in New Zealand. But it wasn't easy! This was yet another journey fraught with anxiety. The boarding school was reserved strictly for New Zealanders in the first year, so he had to do a homestay assigned by the school. It was in a lovely little cabin, away from the main house, owned by an elderly couple. It was nestled in a mature forest of fern, creepers and bramble. It looked like a picture postcard. You could hear the train rumble in the distance which added to its charm. The entire family fell in love with it instantly, but what we didn't anticipate was moss that thrived in damp conditions. The cabin was damp and my son soon developed respiratory problems. We were frequently having to pay close attention to his health.

But, like my daughter, my son soon learnt how to manage his own problems. But, it didn't stop me from worrying. I worried about him finding his way to squash meets that took him to far-flung places, and him getting back to his cabin after dusk, waiting at deserted bus stops in the middle of nowhere. I imagined him lost in a jungle having moved out from the comfort of our living room in urban Singapore. But he managed. He enjoyed the training sessions, tournaments and venues that took him to different parts of Auckland. In awe, he sent us pictures of some of the tournament venues set in picturesque and tranquil environs. He also discovered his passion for history, and started reading widely. He took things in his stride and enjoyed the adventure but one evening a year later, I received a call from him imploring me in a soft grave tone that he wanted to come home. It was a heart-wrenching moment but I had to tell him that it would be best for him to stay and complete his "A" levels. The subtext of my gentle response was: suck it up, and do what you have to do. He did stay, finished his "A" levels and received several awards for squash. After which he came home to do his National Service, mandatory for all Singaporean males, before going on to read law at the University of Manchester, and Master of Laws at University College London, in the United Kingdom.

Ironically, we paid more attention to our children when they were away. We were more vigilant about ensuring they grow up with the right values, out of fear of losing them to bad company, drugs or negligent caregivers and guardians. My husband and I took turns visiting them. We spoke to their teachers and their coaches regularly, instead of waiting to be summoned as in Singapore. For the children, going away to school was great for their overall growth: they learnt to be more independent and confident. But over time, we began to realise that we could no longer dictate what they should or should not do. They had strong beliefs and opinions, and we needed to learn how to talk to them. We needed to present the pros and cons and consider different perspectives, before we presented them with our own opinions. We had to leave some of the decision making to them. We learnt to let go of the apron strings incrementally, let them make their own mistakes and grow from that experience under our close watch. We just needed to be around to help them pick themselves up if they needed us.

I remember the first time I left home, to pursue my university education, after graduating from the Institute of Education in Singapore. I was already in my mid-twenties but I led a sheltered life in my teenage years. But in spite of it, I eventually found the courage to leave home in pursuit of a university education. The memory of parents or grandparents, moving away from the familiar into the unknown in search of a better life, inspires confidence in a young person.

My own decision—to go to Canada to pursue my university education—was partly influenced by a former classmate who lived in Winnipeg with her family. I used to correspond with her regularly. Her description of the prairies, white and pristine with winds howling like hyenas in the middle of the night, threatening to blow into homes that were double-glazed and fortified to keep out the chill, captured my imagination. But it never crossed my mind to study in a place so isolated from the east. So when three of my colleagues, who were fellow teachers in River Valley High School, applied to study in Winnipeg, I was surprised. They convinced me that I was going nowhere in my career, that as a secondary school teacher, with just my "A" levels, I was in a dead-end job. I needed to arm myself with a university degree if I wanted to have a fighting chance at the workplace. It was not an easy decision to make because I had never been away from home. My vice principal sat me down one day and spoke to me about "opportunity costs." He was prepared with the numbers to discourage me from leaving the education service. Strangely, his dollar talk, from beginning to end, pushed me in the opposite direction. The more he spoke, the greater was my resolve to seek the intangible benefits that could possibly emerge from new experiences, new friends and the lure of the unknown.

I applied for an overseas Ministry of Education endowment grant which was approved within a week. It was as if the universe was conspiring to send me away on an adventure. My dad did not object, even before he knew I was going to get the Ministry of Education government aid, he said he would support me as long as he was able to work. He seemed confident to let me go. There were no "ifs," no "buts," no issues with money, even though we didn't have much. Some friends and relatives tried to discourage my dad from sending me to Canada. They said I would pick up smoking and drinking (they hadn't yet heard about the psychedelic drug LSD which was all the rave, in the west, at that time). And they predicted I would lead a promiscuous, western way of life, but he brushed them off. You got a place in university? Then go... so I did, but not without reservations. The wheels of the aircraft were barely up off the tarmac at Changi International Airport when my heart grew heavy, and all I wanted to do was to stop the aircraft from climbing, and run home. But it was too late. Before long we were cruising above the clouds. It would take more than twenty-four hours to reach Winnipeg or "Winterpeg," as the locals called it. Living away from home challenged me at all levels, but I never felt more alive.

Away from home, there was freedom from parental anxieties and concerns. I was exposed to an eclectic life, similar in essence—but different in unimaginable ways—to Kampong Bahru where I grew up. It became clearer to me that things were not always black or white. I had to confront the grey areas that life away from home presented to me. There were respectful and friendly Goths clothed in all-black, wearing heavy mascara and punk hairstyles, who rocked to heavy metal music. There were the feminists who protested aggressively at the slightest hint of male chauvinism, even if you were a professor. There was a male professor with a ponytail and ear studs who was always punctual and methodical in his delivery. There was nothing "hippie" about him. There were the transvestites, lesbians and gays who fought for their rights and demanded their fair share of respect. There were the "native Indians" displaced from their homes who kept to themselves. They would emerge on Friday evenings, mostly with their heads down, and gaze sweeping the floor. We were told that Fridays were when they got their student allowances that they would blow on alcohol and drugs. They did not appear comfortable on campus, unlike the Canadians of European descent whose families had established themselves mostly in farming communities in Manitoba. They contributed to the campus buzz. They were bursting with social energy. Besides attending classes, they would make new friends, some would get drunk on spirits and high on drugs at campus socials, go on dates, picnics, skiing trips and road trips around the lakes and forests on the weekends and public holidays. Many took their social lives and leisure activities as seriously as their academic achievements. Then there were the foreign students—most of the Asians hung together. They ate together. Attended classes together. Studied together, and aced the examinations together. Some, like me, were attracted to the diversity on campus. We befriended students and professors from the different pockets of life and were invited into their lives. There were visits to farms. We got a taste of horse riding. We shoveled hay to feed goats and cows, and grains to chickens and geese in the manger, on wintry mornings, at minus 30 degrees Celsius. We learnt to ski, but mostly it was one giant effort at pulling ourselves out of the snow after numerous tumbles and falls. There were Christmas and Hanukkah parties where I first tasted wild rice salads, rare steaks, Ukrainian red borscht soup and blueberry cheesecake.

Being a long way from home allowed me to socialize and form friendships without fear of judgment. I sprouted wings and allowed myself those short bursts of flight, like a duck from a pond. I made friends with local Canadians, and with others from Europe and Asia. The diversity stretched my imagination. Many people would strike up a conversation with me to learn more about South Asia, assuming that I was from India. Their initial response to my nationality was usually one of shock, as they believed Singapore was a city somewhere in China, or an island near China.

The distance from home also allowed me to listen to my heart without fear of criticism. I found my soulmate on campus to share my life with. The man who would be my husband and I were on-and-off friends on campus for four years because we moved in different social circles. I still remember the defining moment, when I spotted my husband from the bus on my way to university. It was the spring of 1986. I was in my final year and I hadn't seen him for some time. We had parted company in our second year, pursuing our own dreams and goals. Now he looked strangely forlorn and burdened as he walked towards the bus stop, head down, oblivious of the bus he had just missed. Something stirred within me to reach out to him. Little did I realise then that he was indeed weighed down. That afternoon, our paths crossed. We were both headed in the same direction. I was a final year honours student reading English Literature at the University of Manitoba and headed for class. Since he had just missed the bus I was on, upon reaching my destination, I waited for him, eager to meet a my friend I hadn't seen for ages. We got to talking.

I learnt that he had received a scholarship to do his Masters in

Economics at the University of Toronto. He had made a trip by bus from Winnipeg to Toronto the day before to receive his scholarship, and to have a chat with his supervisor on his research interest. Apparently, while waiting for his turn to talk to his supervisor, which took a lot longer than expected, it struck him that the atmosphere in the university was cold and impersonal. So when it was his turn to meet his supervisor, he rejected the scholarship and took the next bus back to Winnipeg. He hadn't slept for forty-eight hours. He had just rejected one of the top universities in Canada and was headed to the University of Manitoba to apply for a scholarship to do his masters there instead. Having done summer courses at the University of Manitoba, he was familiar with the professors and research assistants. He got a scholarship to do his Masters in Economics at the University of Manitoba within the week.

We had some very interesting and intense conversations. We could speak about anything for hours—from philosophy to politics, our families, and where we would like to call home. Our romance blossomed. There seemed to be an invisible hand steering the course of these serendipitous life events.

So, how did my Malayalee dad respond to the prospective groom who was a Singaporean of Punjabi Sikh origin? I left Winnipeg for Singapore approximately four months ahead of Manmindar, as he had his dissertation to complete. It was my birthday. That day, just before catching the taxi to the airport, Manmindar surprised me with a lovely gift of perfumed talcum that came with a white fluffy powderpuff and a bottle of body lotion. It was not just a birthday present but also a "see you soon in Singapore" gift. The fragrance had a powerful lingering effect. It transported me to a bed of lush lavender fields. It was then that he told me he had made arrangements with his older brother, Sukh, to pick me up from my home in Singapore, to go and meet his parents. I agreed. The day arrived, and I got ready, bathing myself in the lavender lotion. Moments before leaving for his parents' home, the bottle of lotion slipped from my hand and crashed onto the floor. It smashed into smithereens together with my heart. What remained of the lotion was its fragrance that filled the entire room. It was a devastating sight. Though I was not generally superstitious, I felt uneasy. I cleaned up the mess quietly, wondering what the evening held for me at his parents' home.

In the meantime, the moment I arrived in Singapore, I spoke at length about Manmindar to my mum. She was delighted, but I didn't have the courage to break the news to my dad. I was worried about his reaction somehow. The day my dad heard the news from my mum, he looked deeply concerned. Though he didn't breathe a word, I could feel the fire emerging from his eyes. It was unnerving. I wished his silence meant consent. I couldn't be sure, but I just decided to take it to be a "yes." My mum wanted to look at his pictures, and she asked me a million questions about him, wanting to get to know him better before he arrived. With half a resounding consent, I agreed to go ahead and meet Manmindar's parents as planned by the prospective groom. They were both lovely. They welcomed me warmly to their flat in Lorong 1, Tao Payoh. And after some sweet black tea whisked with condensed milk, Manmindar's brother Sukh and I left the premises, feeling relieved and pleased that all was well.

September arrived soon, and it was time for Manmindar to come home after having completed his dissertation and *viva voce*. My parents and my uncle Chith, my mum's older brother, looked forward to meeting him. We were celebrating *Onam* at my uncle's place. Onam was a festival that Malayalees in Kerala celebrated to give thanks to the crops they had harvested that season, but we urbanites in Singapore still carried on the tradition. It was a Sunday, and it was deemed to be a perfect time to meet the prospective groom. But Manmindar got cold feet. He had just landed in Singapore, in the morning, after a grueling twenty-four hours or more on the plane. He wanted to make a good impression, and here I was getting all excited for him to meet an entire village that included my cousins, uncles, aunts and friends for *Onam sadhya,* or feast. I was nuts.

When I told my family that he may not come to lunch after all, everyone was disappointed. But my dad spoke up for the first time. He said Manmindar's reluctance to meet us didn't augur well, as it was a sign of a lack of commitment. Then, looking straight into my eyes, he asked me if his parents approved. I said yes, confidently. I didn't have reasons to doubt them.

I could see that my dad, however, was anxious as it must have brought back some horrifying memories of my brother, at eighteen, being chased around the block by a gang of Punjabi men who wanted to beat him up, all because he was dating a girl from the Sikh community. Though this episode had taken place some ten years back, I could see how memories were fresh, not just for my dad but my brother as well. My brother was more upfront: "Are you sure about this, Shal?" he whispered, looking just as anxious. I just knew that all their fears would melt away once they got to know Manmindar.

Eventually the prospective groom mustered enough courage to meet the entire village. He was quiet and overwhelmed, as he was not just meeting my immediate family, but also my cousins and our close friends. It was brutally unnerving for him, though I was relaxed and confident because I had been talking about Manmindar to my family and friends for four months while waiting for him at home.

Manmindar soon became a regular guest at my home. He would visit us every evening and enjoy meals cooked by my mum. Then he would go home and oblige his mum who would have also cooked for him. He ate two dinners, every night, and fortunately he managed to keep fit and wiry, as he was completely devoted to cross-country running upon his return to his home. He loved running for miles. But while he grew on my family, I started getting mixed signals from his parents. I was surprised to hear that they were not too keen for their son to be getting married so soon after his graduation. He and I had just taken out a home loan for an apartment we both fell in love with in City Towers. Manmindar had a job by then with DBS Bank, and I was teaching at Raffles Junior College. We were ready to settle down. But his parents wanted us to wait. They started coming up with excuses and reasons for delaying the wedding. Their reaction took me completely by surprise—they never once had betrayed any reluctance, hostility or animosity, in my presence. Visions of the broken bottle and the heady scent of lavender kept clouding my judgment. I began to harbour doubts that led to a number of skirmishes between Manmindar and me.

Gradually, Manmindar won his parents over by agreeing to a Sikh wedding ceremony at the *Gurudwara,* or temple, as his parents requested. My parents were fine with the arrangement, but my mum wanted a little Hindu ceremony, too. This meant two religious ceremonies, followed by a reception at the hotel. Well, as a dutiful daughter and an edgy daughter-in-law waiting to move into our new apartment, I agreed. I wanted us to get on with our life together. While plans were underway for a Sikh wedding, his parents, unexpectedly, one day announced that it would be fine for us to have only a Hindu wedding. No Sikh wedding! That simplified things. So, then there was a mad rush to look for a Hindu temple, and a hotel to host our wedding guests for a reception, as we wanted to get married a year later, in December 1987. I am not sure why my parents-in-law changed their minds, but it wasn't important. In accordance to Punjabi tradition, I was given a dowry of gold jewelry and sets of Punjabi suits and *sarees* by my parents-in-law, which was a pleasant surprise. They were also gracious in that they seemed to enjoy every bit of the Hindu ceremony and participated fully in the reception. My new husband could not stop his father from making a speech at the wedding reception. He was at the lectern, against his son's wishes, but he did bless us. So, that's how the story goes. I ended up getting married to a university mate whom I met one day in Canada, just as autumn was about to display its colours in all its magnificence.

Attending university away from home was intellectually and socially stimulating. It provided me an eclectic space that challenged all that I believed and knew. It made me think more deeply about my own identity, and I saw myself through new lenses... lenses of those who had first encounters, for instance, with a Singaporean South Asian student in an English literature or philosophy class. Most Asian students in the 1980s gravitated towards the hard sciences, business or computer science modules as those disciplines were perceived to provide greater returns on investment. And here was I, appreciating e. e. cummings, Plath, Hughes and the like. The first reaction at any of the English Literature courses was the same. Course mates and tutors alike would look at me as if I was in the wrong place, and murmur politely, not to me directly, but in my general direction: "This is an honours English seminar." *Hmmm... she's still here! Maybe she doesn't understand English that well.* Some would repeat the statement more loudly and emphatically.

Encounters such as these were amusing, but humiliating when peers or lecturers expressed their surprise that I could write and speak in English. In my American Poetry honours English class, my first assignment was a piece of literary criticism of a poem. My professor, then, expressed emphatically that we would not be able to find any notes or criticisms on the poem: "So, you will be doing the criticism from scratch, without assistance. It's a test of your literary appreciation skills! If you get a failing grade on the test, I am afraid you would have to leave this honours course immediately." I felt affronted. I thought, *Really, this must be a test especially designed for me.* It was not uncommon for Canadians at that time to think that Asians, in general, could hardly write or speak in English.

They probably envisioned us living in treetops to avoid tigers and other wild animals. It was hilarious. They were curious. They wanted to get to know me. I was considered exotic. Aceing my first English literature test was a game-changer. They looked at me with renewed interest, and even more so, my professor who was himself a published poet. "I just love the way you looked at the poem, Shalini. It was refreshing. You are going to be a writer one day." What? Really? I did what I always do—ruminate for days on the literary pieces I had to write on. I would sleep on it, think about it. I just simply loved the rub. It made me think about life—my life, my relationships. I would lose my sleep over the existential questions, and enjoyed the learning as never before. Given the context, I did not attach much value to those words, but it sure did plant seeds of my ambition to be a writer.

What, I wonder, inspires decisions to leave the known for the unknown? My dad embraced the feeling of "not knowing," when he left his homeland, with openness to receive the many gifts that life presents us. Often, we don't see them for what they are. They are sometimes too subtle, obscure or undiscernible because we are focused more on what can go wrong, and what may scuttle our mission. When dad chose to board the SS *Rajulla* and sail to what was then a small inconsequential island, nestled at the end of the Malayan Peninsula, I wondered what his thoughts had been.

Knowing my dad, I figured he must have embarked on the journey with great enthusiasm and anticipation. He recognized life's gifts with gratitude. The gift was the opportunity to make things happen and to start life anew. His mind was free from dark thoughts and biases which allowed him to take the plunge into the unknown. "Not knowing," I guess, is exciting when you start the journey with a child's mind—eager to learn, eager to explore and ready for an adventure, taking the good with the bad. You bear with the discomfort and hardship because it gives you the opportunity to create new beginnings. He would not have dwelt on the crippling possibility of failure. In his mind there would be setbacks that just needed to be handled and tackled. It would have made him feel alive. You feel the rush; the pulse quickens, skips a beat and gradually tapers before it picks up again, at the next new opportunity.

Chapter 15
NOT KNOWING

TIME SOMETIMES HAS A way of distorting memories. I realized that the powerful image of my dad, unconscious and hooked up to defibrillators, had sent me reeling in different directions. Sadness, guilt and regret took on a life of its own that I had little control of. One rainy day, some years after the passing of my dad, I found my mum going through the old photo albums. Joining her, I was amazed by how happy my dad looked in all the pictures—carrying the toddlers at home, at the beach, at the Botanic Gardens or on our holidays abroad mostly in Malaysia and Australia. He looked fulfilled. My doubts about my dad, having to assume the role of a grandparent against perhaps his wishes, took a tumble. Photographs don't lie. These were taken before PhotoShop became a thing! And my dad was not one known to pose and pretend to be happy.

He appeared to be a happy retiree. Now, at sixty-two, I found it was difficult for me to walk in his footsteps. Even making somewhat risk-free, safe choices—from the familiar into the unknown—was demanding too much "think time" from me. Choosing retirement over reemployment was a difficult choice. The retirement that I had looked forward to many years ago felt like a bottomless black hole, now that it had arrived. It left me with a sinking feeling. It felt far safer to leverage on my past achievements, skills and knowledge, because I felt that my accomplishments defined me. I had worked as a teacher, teacher-mentor and teacher-educator for a full thirty-nine years of my adult life. Why would I walk away from a lifetime's work that was generally fulfilling? But I felt the need for change: to free myself from the "dos" and "don'ts" and "shoulds" and "shouldn'ts" that work imposed. Familiarity, even when it is stultifying, is difficult to shake off, mostly because we are all creatures of habit. It would be easier to stick to a routine, even if it had become stale and ungratifying, than to create a new pattern. But I needed to sprout wings and explore other interests and options. I needed to exercise my creative energy. What was stopping me was fear. Fear of not knowing how I would respond to the absence of a ready-made, structured routine and schedules imposed by work.

I could see how I was no entrepreneur like my dad; I had a stable government job for thirty-nine years—we called it the "iron rice bowl." I didn't have to grapple with ways and means to sustain my business. In good times and bad, there were students to teach and teachers to mentor. Did I have to go looking for work? Not really. In spite of the various challenges and heartaches, in spite of everything, there was a stable income to put more than just food on the table. All that it demanded was diligence, and I could have cruised along this route, if I wanted to, for the next ten years. I wondered if my dad had gone through a similar dilemma when he retired and gave up his business. *He must have,* I thought to myself although, private as he was, he would have kept his fears to himself. Most of my family and friends wanted me to stay in service because the pay was good and it was familiar terrain. Would my dad have wanted me to retire? I could drift comfortably for the next five to ten years, until I wanted to call it a day. I could then pursue my dream of learning to paint or whatever else my heart desired. But would it be too late? Five to ten years is a long time. I might have lost my shine, by then. My spirit may be raring to break boundaries and create new grounds. But my faculties and senses may not be able to keep up with the fire within.

If I do retire, how would I shape my future? What would I want it to look like? What would I fill the days with? What if I had grandchildren? Would I want to spend most of the hours in the day looking after them, as my parents did? I wasn't sure. I always loved writing and painting, but I never really got around to doing more of these creative activities because of work commitments. Would I actively seek writing retreats and artistic pursuits to grow in these areas? Will I make myself vulnerable by sharing my writing with the world? There were many unanswered questions. But, it would, most certainly, be easier, to retreat into a comfortable cocoon, away from the watchful eyes of the public, upon retirement. There is comfort in that sort of existence, after all. Ah! The bliss! The peace, the feeling of eternal sleep—but the creative part of me was still in its infancy, waiting to discover itself.

I knew I had to write but I was fearful of public scrutiny and criticism. It was daunting. I drew some inspiration from the prolific American poet, singer and memoirist, Maya Angelou, who humbly confessed: "*Nothing so frightens me as writing, but nothing so satisfies me. It is a matter of taking a few verbs, and some adverbs, some adjectives, nouns, and pronouns, and put(ting) them all together and mak(ing) them bounce.*" If only it was that easy! The prospect of throwing words into the air and juggling with them was as exciting as it was frightening, but take a leaf out of her book of wisdom, I did!

But, as soon as I got comfortable, I would be riddled once again with nagging doubts, excuses, perhaps to avoid getting started. This time, it was about my intention to write: Is it narcissistic, this impulse to write and share my life with the public? I watched an interview with the famous chef, the late Anthony Bourdain, a few months before his death. What he felt about his highly acclaimed travel show seemed like profound guilt. Just talking about how much airtime he was getting as a roving celebrity chef made him uncomfortable. He described the whole act of drawing attention to himself, even as a chef, as narcissistic. I couldn't understand this! His travel shows were the hard work of not just himself but an entire crew, and he gave credibility and social standing to "street food"—the food of ordinary people all over the world. Yet he could not see this.

I was vacillating between fear and doubt, and the opposing sense of wanting to break out of the old mould and do something I actually enjoyed—like write. I couldn't understand where these seeds of fear and doubt could have come from. My dad and most of his generation were fearless. They had the courage and innocence to believe! If you believed in something you just had to do it. Take the plunge!

Fear of criticism and failure, I realized, is deeply embedded in the modern Singaporean psyche. The thought of failure is petrifying. Fear drives many of our decisions and actions. Nothing is ever enough! Top down, we are reminded. We need to do more, accumulate more. Why? Because we are a small nation; because no one owes us a living; because we are surrounded by our enemies waiting to see us fall; because we don't have natural resources; because we can't afford to be a welfare state. Because we need to fend for ourselves.

During the earliest days of Singapore, we lived in perpetual fear of being eaten up by the communists or by our big brothers in the 'hood. We were made to feel like a nut caught in the jaws of a nutcracker. After that, it was the fear of being left behind in the information age, the fear of China rising, the fear of automation threatening to take away our livelihoods. We needed to know more. We needed to do more.

What haunts us now is the fear of being confronted by a Volatile, Uncertain, Complex and Ambiguous (VUCA) world. We put on the warpaint and chant "VUCA, VUCA, VUCA." It has become the tribal chant, from government ministers on down. One would have thought that the daily diet of fear would have prepared us well for the "unknown." But alas, we don't seem to have had enough of it, even though history, legends, myths, fairytales and nursery rhymes should have taught us amply that the world is indeed complex, uncertain and ambiguous. The world is scary, beginning with the expulsion of Adam and Eve from the Garden of Eden, Hansel and Gretel's abandonment in the woods, Humpty Dumpty's fall from a solid brick wall (but we saw that coming: his head was far too big for his body!) to the classic lullaby: rock-a-bye baby on the tree top. And before you know it, down comes baby, cradle and all.

I know we need to learn to embrace the "unknown," problems and all. Kiss as many frogs; take risks, break free from the tyrannical grasp of despots and step up into the golden chariot that could take us to the ball. It should be a great opportunity, should it not, to rethink, recalibrate, reinvent and break free from prescriptive, stultifying and bureaucratic thinking?

The moment I made this commitment to leave, after thirty-nine years in government service, a world of new possibilities was uncovered before me. The decision to retire acted like a catapult. It flung me out of my "comfort zone." I reached out to connect with old friends and old acquaintances who could help me shape my new future. I was still in survival mode. Instead of just relaxing and letting things be, I wanted now, more than ever, to make things happen. I was searching. But why did I need to do that? Why couldn't I, just like my dad did, say, "Enough!" I have made my contributions. It seemed to be time to pass the baton to the younger generation, but still be there to support them when they needed help. But I had to be doing something.

Chapter 16
LET STILLNESS LIGHT YOUR WAY

LIKE MY DAD, I would not have been considered a religious person when I was a young adult. I would stand before the altar and pray, but only occasionally. My visits to the temple were just as rare but it didn't have anything to do with not believing. I did acknowledge the superior presence of something beyond us. But I just gave in to a busy life: working, raising my children, running my errands and doing the needful.

All that changed, however, when I sent my twelve-year-old daughter away to Melbourne for her studies. I felt rudderless. No amount of due diligence to ensure that she was safe gave me the assurance that she would be fine. I needed something more. I remember consulting an astrologer to see if there were any special prayers or *pariharam,* peace offerings, I could do to make amends so that the stars would treat her favourably and protect her. I believed, strange as it may seem, that the position of the planets did have an influence on the life and future of a person! As an adolescent, I read books on palmistry and was inclined to accept to some extent that the lines on your palm indicated your present and future well-being. The lines on the left hand, I read, was what you were born with whereas the lines on the right were what you made out of your life. So, destiny was something that I believed could be altered.

It was strange for me to have taken an interest in astrology and palmistry, because my dad certainly did not believe that the position of the planets could foretell one's destiny. It was customary for astrological charts to be drawn up at the birth of a newborn in Hindu homes and, as my mother and aunt were more prone to follow the traditional ways, my children's charts were made. But whenever we had the astrologer over, my dad would disappear. He didn't believe in it and wouldn't want to listen to the astrologer. He was quite unequivocal in his belief that some of these astrologers were shysters waiting to make a quick buck. He would say all you needed was pure faith, and the will to be captain of your ship. He also had faith that everything would be fine. "All will be well," he would often chime, which I could not understand. I was then critical of my dad because I would visualise in my mind's eye how things could go wrong in a million ways. Unlike me, my dad was driven by all the ways things could work for the better. Even if things did not work out, he knew if one had the strength and tenacity to handle a problem, then it could be averted, minimized or at the least one could learn from it. You had to have faith. That explained his calm in the face of problems of any kind when we were children. He would be as still as the eye of the storm. You wouldn't find him rushing to do things. He would calmly do the needful. Even if he got angry, it was only because he wanted to display his displeasure. He knew what exactly made him angry. He did not carry the baggage with him or unleash his frustration on innocent bystanders. I realized that I didn't have such indomitable trust and faith in the universe, and as a parent I felt vulnerable.

So, feeling we had to make amends for past karma, my husband and I consulted the priest. He said we needed to carry out prayers to *Lord Ganesha*, the remover of obstacles, and *Lord Dhashnamoorthy*, who represented educational development and career advancement. My Western education and logical mind did not, surprisingly, stand in the way of me carrying out the priest's instructions. I did what I had to do for the safe passage of my twelve-year-old daughter who was to leave home for Melbourne to pursue her studies. I made the prayers, every Thursday, for nine weeks. I did them without fail, and carried on with the temple visits thereafter. The priest would chant the mantras for ten minutes, but it gave me solace. I would then sit quietly for a couple of minutes more in the temple. It helped me still my mind and tame my wild imagination that was predisposed to conjuring up worst-case scenarios. Was I using religion as a crutch? I suppose I was. I felt too small, powerless and vulnerable to stand on my own, even though I was in my mid-forties. So the weekly temple visits were calming. They helped smooth my frazzled nerves and gave me greater clarity to deal with my life.

However, at fifty-eight, I started learning to meditate and still my mind. I started with baby steps of five minutes, which progressed gradually from ten to fifteen to twenty and twenty-five minutes. And now I am at a comfortable thirty minutes, though I am able to occasionally still my mind and enjoy the calm for forty-five minutes.

How did I come to meditate? It just happened, but the circumstances that led to my meditation practice were strange. It was the end of 2012, my husband and I were invited to a wedding in Kuala Lumpur (KL), and so was my brother. We drove up to KL while my brother flew from Singapore with an uninvited guest, a buddy of his from law school, Dinesh, who would crash the wedding party. At cocktails, it was amusing watching two grown men, Suresh and Dinesh, having fun with the introductions as the hosts wondered who this unknown guest was.

We had fun as my brother and his friend made a witty duo, but one morning at breakfast, our conversation took us to life and work, and how we could make it more fulfilling and meaningful. Dinesh spoke with candour about his experiences at work as a CEO, and took me through Stephen Covey's *7 Habits of the Mind for Highly Effective People*. I was amazed at how simply he summarized a whole book on a paper napkin, over morning coffee. His simple yet commonsensical explanation got me reflecting on my own work and my approach to people and life. After coffee, we dropped into a bookshop at the KLCC mall to find Covey's book. Inspired, I bought it. A few minutes later, Dinesh emerged with a gift. It was Paramahansa Yogananda's

Autobiography of a Yogi. On the inside of the book, he wrote, "Here's a treasure trove to carry with you on your journey back from head to heart." It was a spontaneous gesture of friendship, and he told my husband and me to read the book because it had changed his life.

I received the book with, I would admit, some skepticism. I was generally suspicious of self-proclaimed, self-aggrandising yogis, ascetics and preachers, some of whom I felt exploited others at their weakest moments for profit. They often unleashed their dogma when you were at your most vulnerable or when you were least suspecting. Fortunately, Narayana Guru (my dad's guru) and Paramahansa Yogananda were not "living gurus." It made it easier for me to consider the merit of their teachings and what they stood for, objectively, without being swayed by charisma or personality. I was also inherently skeptical, like my dad, of those who proclaimed with pride that *their* way was the *only* way to enlightenment. While I was generally tolerant of such fervent declarations spoken with certitude, I felt that the display of such sentiments was divisive and ultimately harmful and damaging to peace in a world that was highly diverse and multi-dimensional. So, when I received the book, I took it with a healthy dose of skepticism.

In spite of my biases, I suspended judgment and picked up *Autobiography of a Yogi* with an open mind, after we got home from KL. I couldn't put the book down. I was captivated. The anecdotes of the young Yogi's experiences with the mystical sages and gurus, on his journey to self-realisation, stretched my imagination and broadened my vision. A plethora of nuanced perspectives on spiritual life unraveled before me. With each of the young Yogi's experiences with the Perfume Saint, the Tiger Swami, the Levitating Saint, the Sleeping Saint, the Mohammedan Wonder Worker or the everyday postman, I felt my pupils dilate with wonder and awe. I was enthralled. Nothing seemed impossible in this life. While the narrative had a child-like innocence and authenticity that made you want to suspend disbelief, it felt strangely empowering. What was refreshing was that each swami or guru had a personality and spiritual life that was distinctly different. Each had its own purpose to fulfil, in his own way. There was no "one way" of attaining self-knowledge or self-realisation.

While each Saint or Guru brought with him his own philosophy and beliefs on existence and truth, they were all seekers of self-realisation. That was the essence, I think, I found most appealing and humbling. One generation passed on its experiences to the next, and the next and the next, with not the slightest intention to stifle individual expression and exploration. The aim was to liberate seekers of truth to discover their own truth, in their own way. I learnt that the true practice of yoga was meant to be spiritual, and was the science of self-realisation. Greek philosophers, such as Aristotle espoused similar ideas. They proclaimed as Aristotle did that "Knowing yourself is the beginning of wisdom."

Rereading the *Autobiography*, while ruminating on my dad's life, and my relationship with him, made me realise that there was a common thread that appealed to us. Both my dad's guru and the gurus presented in the *Autobiography*, were inclusive in the way they viewed life and the universe. In an attempt to be inclusive, they drew attention to the artificial constructs that lay between East and West, Brahmin and Ezhava, and Christian and Mohammedan, Hindu and Buddhist that prevented man from achieving both inner peace and a harmonious co-existence in this life. It reinforced for me the idea that in order to appreciate a culture or preserve one, you do not need to denounce or denigrate another. It also dawned on me how I had enjoyed a liberal upbringing this far. My father never once imposed his religious or spiritual beliefs on us. Though later in life he used to stand before the altar at home and pray at dawn and dusk and visit temples weekly, he never once summoned us to do the same. To him, it was a personal choice. The liberal upbringing forged a sense of inclusivity in my brother and I. We could walk into a church, Buddhist temple or mosque to light a candle, and find joy in the peace. We had humility enough to acknowledge the presence of an infinite force beyond us that was omniscient and omnipresent. The infinite life force existed in everything, from a stone thoughtlessly kicked around to a grain of sand conveniently overlooked. It was a luxury to have been given the bandwidth to continue seeking and thinking about the inexplicable questions about life and existence.

The Autobiography exemplified, through the experiences of Yogananda, that you have the support of a whole universe in your pursuit of self-realisation. It reminded me of one of Maya Angelou's speeches. In it, she invites everyone not to feel alone in their pursuit of knowledge, wisdom, or even that nerve-wracking interview you have to go to. She says that there's nothing to fear; just bring along everyone who has gone before you—your grandparents, parents, uncles, aunties, uncles, mentors, teachers, saints, yogis, gurus—everyone! You don't have to be alone, and you are not alone. Take them with you. These ideas struck a chord with me. We are indeed the sum of the parts of our treasure trove of knowledge and experiences that went before us.

After I read *The Autobiography of a Yogi*, I passed it on to my husband. He still reads excerpts from the book every day, before bedtime. Why? What did he find so appealing? He who reads historical novels and narratives about extraordinary lives and journeys of men, found this one book satisfying his soul's yearning, perhaps, for the one life in a world divided.

Though I had started reading about the value of yoga, meditation and introspection, I did not put any of it into practice. The ideas floated like clouds in my mind until they were almost forgotten.

A year later, I chanced upon an advertisement in the *Straits Times*. I recognized the cover of the *Autobiography of a Yogi*. It was an invitation to a talk by two disciples of Paramahansa Yogananda on the art of meditation. They were teachers from the Ananda Group. I attended the talk with my mum and husband, eager to learn to meditate. After the talk, my husband and I registered for the weekly Saturday classes. The lessons were invaluable. I learnt to first prepare my body mentally and physically for meditation by doing the energization exercises that disciplined the mind by drawing its attention to different muscle groups from head to toe. There were thirty-nine moves designed to awaken every sinew in the body. While the exercises were simple, the act of focusing on particular muscle groups was a challenge, because the mind invariably has the tendency to drift. It could be as simple as "What's for breakfast?" instead of "This is my left calf muscle. I can feel it tightening now and then relaxing." Next, instead of focusing on my right calf muscle tightening and relaxing, I am having panic attacks thinking about a presentation I have to give in a couple of hours to teachers in a school. The energization exercises helped with my gradual disciplining of my mind to bring to awareness, and remind me of the infinite life force that we all carry with us in every atom of the body. The discipline involves bringing the mind back to the life force within you, every time it strays.

Then, there is the breath that unifies the whole of mankind, regardless who or what you are. I took comfort in the thought that "Tinker, tailor, soldier, sailor, rich man, poor man, beggarman, thief"—everyone and anyone—could understand and learn to appreciate the breath. Inhaling and exhaling are natural, regardless of who or what we are. I learnt about the science of breathing. As you follow your breath, there comes a point when the inhaling breath and exhaling breath meet until all you feel is calm and bliss as body, mind and soul align in harmony. It clears the murky waters so that you can see things for what they are.

I believe that the customs, traditions, rituals and holy books that differentiate us are not meant to divide but enrich our lives. They are a means of providing us with rich perspectives to grow and continue to grow, so that we may become active participants rather than blind followers in our life's journey, willfully participating rather than mindlessly giving in.

Since the beginning of 2014, I have started each day with twenty minutes of energisation exercises followed by the "child's pose" or *Balasana*, as a reminder to remove all social biases and prejudices and to see the world with childlike wonder. And then I sit quietly on my ankles, knees folded in *Vajrasana*. After which I do three rounds of *Maha Mudra,* which prepares me for meditation. I meditate for about thirty minutes on average every day. I start the day with my communion with the infinite spirit within. It could be God, Father in Heaven, Divine Mother, Allah, Supreme Being or the Wisdom of the Universe to some. What's in a name? What matters is this humble acknowledgment: you don't know everything, you can't know everything, and there is so much more that you need to understand and know, beginning with yourself. The Kena Upanishads, written some thousand years ago, summarises this wisdom aptly in the following lines: "I do not think I know it well. Nor do I know that I do not know it. Among us those who know, know it; even they do not know that they do not know."

The Cave

I am a householder.
I have responsibilities and duties.
I should not and ought not to
Seek those sacred quiet spaces
In caves, hidden away,
In distant mountains.

But what I would and can do
Is to seek and steal
Moments of time
In the cave of mine eye.
And, there I shall espy
Who I am...

Chapter 17
DISCOVERING THE UNLIVED LIFE THROUGH ART

WITH MY PRACTICE OF meditation, I begin each day with greater clarity and have since become more aware of the heartbeat in every little thing! I find myself noticing every tree, shrub, blade of grass, flower, sky or mountain. It led to a yearning to capture the way the branches fall and rise through the air in a hundred different permutations. If only I could paint the sun in all its splendour, spreading its orange hues across the dusky blue sky, making its descent into the emerald green sea. My desire to paint was so strong that one day, in spite of my busyness at work, I let my fingers go astray and Googled for art classes in Singapore. One thing led to another, and on the website of Studio Miu Art, I was drawn to an oil painting. It was the silhouette of a lady with inky black hair and dress, paintbrush in hand lighting the canvas with a kaleidoscope of colours. I found the artist and enrolled in her class.

My art teacher, Junkosan, was perfect for me. She did not start with theories, principles and techniques. She started with a childlike simplicity. What do you want to paint? You choose. Search inside yourself; look into your heart. What would you like to paint? Just as spontaneously, I chose to paint a memory that was very close to my heart. It was my first Sakura moment: cherry blossoms pink, white and purple had pushed their way out of hard, dry brown twigs to colour the air, and decorate lives. The air buzzed with hope and new beginnings as *Hanami* parties sprouted spontaneously in parks and gardens in the suburbs of Tokyo. Droves of locals and tourists descended on Shinjuku Goen. Some spilled out of their office buildings in mid-afternoon with their picnic mats, sushi bento sets, bottles of wine, crackers and fries to submerge themselves in hues of pink. There today, gone tomorrow. If you miss it now, you'll never know if you will live another day to encounter this moment again. *Sakura* or cherry blossoms have become a symbol of the transience of life in Japanese culture. The flowers are a surprise party. They stay on the branches but briefly, shedding each petal to decorate the ground before they become part of the earth. It was a maiden experience, and sharing it with my first child, now a young woman, was special. That day there were two girls on a mission. For me, I was chasing a dream. For my daughter, the impetus was to get the *Sakura* moments to her mum.

And so, I chose to paint my first art piece. It was from a photograph of me gazing upwards at a buxom branch of Sakura blooms flushed with pink hues. I posed triumphantly. Then came the next question from my art teacher: would you like to draw on a drawing block paper, or canvas? My first response was to sketch on a drawing block paper, just in case I make mistakes. Also, what if I discover I can't draw it? The drawing block paper, thirty-two cm. by twenty cm., was safe.

So, why then in a split second did I change my mind? I am not sure! I was soon choosing from a stack of linen canvasses. The one I chose was seventy-three cm. by sixty-one cm. "Such audacity!" I muttered to myself. "Where would you like to hang your painting?" asked my teacher in her soft girlish voice, sounding absolutely genuine and confident that this painting would be worth putting up on the wall. I was, of course, amused and skeptical at the teacher's optimism. "In a place with plenty of light or along a corridor with little light?" she went on. Every time Junkosan asked me a question, she would wait for an answer before moving on. She was comfortable waiting. Those were Zen moments prompting thoughts to come from my heart. "Your decision has to come from your heart," she would say.

What did I learn through the process? Why did Junkosan's approach appeal to me? Just like my dad let me be, she encouraged me to dig deep into myself to discover my heart's yearning, and not what one should or should not paint. Painting, I discovered, was so much like writing. When you write inside yourself, you never know where your writing may take you. Similarly, there can be surprising outcomes when you dabble in paint. My art teacher encouraged me to follow my intuition. She didn't want to hamper me with the mechanics. She wanted it to be a process of discovery. She didn't want me to be too careful. She would slap paint all over my pristine canvas. I would gasp! It felt like an aberration! It was painful but I learnt to gradually accept that it was fine as she taught me how to work the "mistake" away.

She showed me how to notice the effects of the "mistake" on canvas. "There is no such thing as a permanent irreversible mistake," she would say. I needn't be afraid. Almost every problem is rectifiable on canvas. I realise as I write and paint that I am building on the foundation blocks taught me by my dad. The choices I make seem to emerge from my upbringing. I am not used to being overly restricted with fixed structures. I thrive when there is flexibility for my individual expression and growth.

The canvas became my palette. It was a playground. I could have fun in it. It was a garden. I could plant and replant anything on it. "The mistakes you make on canvas add to the richness and depth of a painting," my teacher would say. "It's no longer a shallow pool of water you are gazing into, but a sea or ocean, bottomless and reflecting depths of meaning as layers after layers unfold—now green, now blue, turquoise, emerald, lapis lazuli, bronzy black, muddy, grey—inviting in its brilliance, sparkling like a gem, mysteriously deep and threatening all at once."

I am now ten paintings older and richer. I have moved from painting landscapes to portraits to figure sketching. Today, however, my art teacher tells me to be more careful. "Watch how the light falls." She talks to me about the classical brush strokes. "Don't push the brush into the canvas. It's the skin you are painting. Use a feather touch; the paint is translucent, let the skin glow. Let the warmth shine through."

I wondered how I could have missed an interest that lay dormant in me for so many years. It brought me back to the time when I was ten. I entered an ESSO colouring competition. I used Staedtler coloured pencils to paint a picture of a tiger in its natural habitat. My mum and dad were elated when I won an ESSO gas stove, because at that time we were using an old kerosene stove to cook our food at home. We had to collect the prize from a provision shop in Balestier Road, some distance from where we lived. I remember my dad and me catching a bus, and walking for miles after we alighted before we got our hands on the stove. From then onwards, we used gas stoves to cook our food. I felt proud, and so did my dad. He looked positively happy that day, but back in the day, no one would have thought about drawing or painting as a means of making a living.

When I was a student in secondary school, art was put on the back burner. I wonder where that attitude came from. There was almost nothing memorable about art lessons, but once, I had to paint a pineapple for a Secondary Two final examination. The pineapple stood before me. I wondered how I was going to capture its imprint. I sketched something that looked like a pineapple. Then I painted it. I remember not being happy with the colours. I thought to myself, *this is a mistake*. I remember adding more colours to correct the wrong. My brush went *criss-cross, criss-cross* to form a trellis of triangles. In the end it was a horrible mess! Where did the golden yellow pineapple go? I thought to myself, *This is a sure fail!* But I wasn't worried about repercussions from my parents, teachers or other students. "You failed art?" It was always fine to fail art. Nobody took art seriously. Maybe there was a feeling that anybody could draw or paint. A week later, when the teacher released the results of the art examination to the class, I was shocked! I topped the class! That horrible dirty painting had appealed to one judge: the marker.

But I knew not the reasons. Though I loved going to art galleries as an adult, I didn't pick up a brush again until forty-seven years later.

Both writing and painting, inside myself, has put me in touch with my creative self. They complement my daily meditation practice and have helped me achieve a greater appreciation of myself and nature. I see the infinite life force in everything around me: people, places and things. Although in spite of the daily meditation practice, I was still occasionally prone to bouts of disappointment and despair, the arts taught me to be calmer and more even-minded. I have become less reactive and more able to see people and relationships for what they are. I am also more willing to suspend my judgment of others and let things go.

So began my journey to capture memories of beautiful moments with my family on the bare canvas and blank page. And not dwell on the dark spots that have a way of consuming life. I want my children to be able to remember the moments in those spaces that lifted our spirits.

Chapter 18
WRITING IN THE DARK—MEDITATIVE WRITING

WHAT INSPIRED ME TO write this memoir about my dad? I am not sure, but it's been festering and brewing inside me. Since my dad's passing fourteen years ago, I've been writing in my head, over and over again. Most of the moments I rehearsed writing in my head were dark and depressing. I never really shook off the images of my dad hooked up to heart monitors, and breathing and feeding through tubes. I still heard hints of his guttural wail making its way through a veil of clouds. I would then scribble my pain in notebooks and scraps of paper, never to be found again. Sometimes, my thoughts got lost in a sea of words and remained only as thought bubbles.

I remember the day when I unearthed a stack of programmes of Indian dance performances that we had attended as a family in the 1970s. My mum had collected and kept them as souvenirs. The various Indian dance costumes looked resplendent on the dancers in the various poses they struck. I looked for my dad's name in the "Acknowledgments," but in vain. Where was his name? I was angry and saddened. I wanted to publicise and acknowledge his work posthumously, but that would mean getting in touch with all these dancers. Where would I find them? They could be dead for all I know. Then what? It infuriated me that, though these dancers had the decency to invite us to their performances, they did not care to acknowledge the artisan behind the costumes that made the pages and stages pop with vitality and beauty.

But like a thunderbolt, memories of my dad knocked me off my high horse. I, too, perhaps might have not been any different. What have I done, I wondered, to celebrate what my father stood for? That was the turning point. I decided I would start writing my dad's memoir.

Not enough is said about the quiet and unassuming ones amongst us who make sacrifices to raise others, and who have no qualms celebrating the successes of others without envy. They know not they are the true heroes who have laid the ground for others to flourish. My dad would never have thought himself a hero. True heroes like my dad drift in and out of life, from day to day, unnoticed and unappreciated. I wanted my dad to know he was a true hero, worthy of celebration. I needed to pay a long overdue tribute to my dad.

The year before, in December, feeling somewhat destabilised at my impending retirement, I had reached out to a friend, Marion Neubronner, who is a corporate coach and Asian entrepreneur. After thirty-nine years of toil, I could not just do nothing; I could not just kick back, sip on coffee or wine (depending on the time of day), contemplate life and enjoy my freedom from routine, deadlines, meetings, and to-do lists that keep sprouting like Hydra's heads. I was almost desperate to find something to fill my time. I was, perhaps, hoping to pick up where we had left off some five years earlier, when Marion told me to consider doing one of her courses—to train as a coach. Now, Marion congratulated me on my decision to retire. "You have given enough of yourself. You need to do something for yourself now. What do you really want for yourself? What would make you truly happy? If money is not an issue, what would it be?" It was a difficult conversation, mostly because there was no fire in my belly propelling me forward one way or other. It was lukewarm. It could be this. It could be that. It could be anything, really. "But what do you really want to do? What makes you truly happy?" I paused. I hesitated. And I wondered at my response. It seemed like a simple question, but it took me awhile before I blurted, "I want to be able to write, to publish, to tell a story about my dad, though I love reading and writing poems." "What do you have fun doing that you want to do more of?" "I have just discovered the joys of oil painting. I would love to do more of that as well: write, paint."

"How much writing have you done so far?" "I have written some poems." But four years ago, I was inspired to write again, when I attended a writing retreat organised by the Singapore Writing Institute at the English Language Institute of Singapore, where I worked as a Master Teacher or Teacher Educator. It was a three-week writing retreat for teacher leaders who taught English language. The facilitator was a teaching fellow from the National Writing Project in the United States. He inspired confidence. He had some really cool strategies to get me to write inside myself. The more I wrote, the more I wanted to carry on writing. At every retreat thereafter, for four years, be it as a facilitator or writing coach, I wrote alongside the teacher participants. I have since published a few poems in one of our internal publications. "I want to write about my dad. I will start when I retire." "Why wait 'til you retire, Shalini? Why not start now? Why wait?" was her response. "I am trying to understand your reluctance to write. What's blocking the flow?" She ignored my answer when I told her I had little time. We all know time is something you will find when there is a fire in the belly propelling you forward. *Why was I not prioritising my writing?* I always felt that post-retirement would provide me with an eternity of time to do the many things I have always wanted to do, like write. Why did I need to start right away? "Because of death." Marion's response was blunt, but honest. She was right, of course. "We can never be sure that we'll live another day to tell our tale. The story might go unheard." I listened in quiet amusement to the stark truth.

Marion continued, "Let me help you get started. I am spending the weekend with my niece at a resort in Johor. Why don't you join me? You can spend your time writing your first chapter. Thereafter, you'll send me your chapters as you finish them." It sounded like a great plan, though I felt daunted and strangely overwhelmed. I started expressing my second excuse: "I think I need to attend a writing retreat first, to get some tips and inspira–" I had barely ended my sentence when she quipped, "You have all the knowledge you need to write. You have to just sit yourself down to write. Come with me to Johor." I agreed. I looked forward to the day, but suddenly, the morning of the trip, I was struck by a bad bout of gastrointestinal flu. *Could this be psychosomatic?* I thought to myself. I decided to turn up no matter what, but the fever and frequency of toilet visits left me little choice. I rang Marion on the morning of the day we were supposed to depart. She sounded suspicious, but resigned. She wished me well and was about to hang up when I blurted a promise to her, "Marion, I'll send you my first chapter by the end of the month. I will start writing now." And so I started writing my memoir.

There were times I would write as if in a trance: I could hear crickets and the distant roar of traffic reduced to a purr, the crackling of a plastic wrapper, the distinct whiff of chocolate mint toffee. My fingers would glide along the page, making imprints in ink. My eyes would drop and rise in meditative silence in response to a memory that would stop for me. I would, then, be able to capture all its beauty in stillness.

Writing without a plan is like writing in the dark. Try doing the *Vrikshasana,* or tree pose, in the dark with your eyes closed. In darkness, balance on one leg with both hands stretched upwards as if reaching out for the skies. Then close your eyes. Unless your focus is razor sharp, it has a destabilising effect. The tree threatens to uproot. Pitch blackness throws you off. Just as the eyes are used to seeing, the mind seeks a plan before writing takes place. It's all part of the conditioning. Writing without a plan is almost counterintuitive, but you need to sit yourself down and write, and just enjoy getting lost in space without worrying about the destination. Just write until you get used to not having any expectations of yourself as a writer. You need to lose the sense of self, and suppress that internal critic that twitches at every word. Just write "in the moment;" write inside yourself; write because you have a story to tell—and I did. I suspended judgment. I got the internal critic to quieten down. I just wrote. I did not plan what I was going to say. I let the writing lead the way. Having rehearsed the writing in my head all those years, I started this memoir with the "awkward hug," because that was the moment that triggered questions about my relationship with my dad.

With every word, phrase, sentence and paragraph, the pages rolled out as the remembrance of every banal moment lit up the page—moments forgotten, moments buried that had filled our lives from day to day. My dad's whistling of his favourite Malayalam tune, of a girl of his dreams with dark kohl eyes shaped like a conch shell, drifted from the deep recesses of the mind. His deep penetrating eyes met mine. Those eyes could turn daggers just as quickly, after a warm welcome, if confronted with the slightest trace of injustice. I could hear the quiet rhythm of the wheel of the Singer sewing machine spinning in the day, dad's feet gently pedalling. The aroma of spices drifted in from the fifteen vegetarian dishes with unique flavours, waiting to be savoured: roasted coconut, yoghurt mixed with turmeric, *asafoetida* blended with potatoes and snake gourde, ginger and lemon pickles roasted in *masala*, and for a sweet note, broken green *gram* and roasted cashew nuts cooked in coconut milk and *jaggery* were laid out on the dining table to celebrate nature's gifts with gratitude on *Onam*, a harvest festival celebrated in Kerala. There was pride and joy, especially when we had guests joining us for family festivities. It was never about what we did not have; it was about what we did have, and what we could give. It was never about not owning a television set like the neighbours who proudly displayed a television in their living rooms. It almost always was about relationships and dad's role as a provider, bringing everyone together around the culinary delights and personal space we shared. From nowhere emerged these precious memories, almost forgotten, as I wrote in meditative silence.

With every word I write, I have strangely discovered my own fears of retiring into the twilight of my life. My fear of abandonment, the fear of losing identity and self-worth, the fear of being crippled by disease and impending death—the eyes get fixated. Regrets loom larger than life. But writing broke the spell. I sought to look through lenses other than my own. Frame by frame, I recalibrated my views until I began to see things for what they are. I started my journey with regret, with the image of my dad, abandoned and helpless. But with every recollection and every imprint of the word turned inwards, that image of my dad, in conscious unconsciousness, became a blurry cloud drifting into oblivion. I began to realise that black blotches have a way of filling the canvas with shadow, until all is lost in gloom. Writing has allowed me to gradually come out of the shadows. It has become clearer to me now that I need to leave a legacy for my children and nephews and their children's children. The next generation needs to understand the lives of their grandparents and great-grandparents. There will be stories to tell from the books I've written. There will be paintings on walls from memories I've captured. Every word, every brushstroke will breathe of a life lived and loved.

But in order to publish my memoir, I couldn't just continue writing meditatively. The chapters had to cohere; the grammar had to be correct and enhance meaning; the words had to come to life and grip the reader; the structure had to sustain the reader's interest. There were endless concerns to ensure that I did justice to my dad, and to the reader who would, hopefully, take away a leaf or two from the memoir.

After ten chapters, I was stuck. I had run out of ideas. So I sent Marion my ten-chapter manuscript, because I needed a response. She responded that I was now ready for a writing coach. She introduced me to two people who she said might be able to assist me with feedback. One had volunteered to read my manuscript for free, and promised to give me a response, and the other was a professional writing teacher in the United States. I sent them both ten chapters of my manuscript. I didn't hear from the volunteer. He did not acknowledge my email with the manuscript, either. I waited a few weeks. Puzzled at the silence, I decided to resend the email with a polite note stating that I was sorry for not having sent the manuscript earlier and was looking forward to a response. There was a similar deafening silence. I wondered for days what the reason could've been. *Was it that bad? Maybe he was plain bored? Actually, who would want to read about someone's poor dad? In an age where a person's worth is measured by the billions of dollars he makes, what are people drawn to?* Apart from the lifestyles of the rich and famous and rich crazy Asians, we would gravitate towards autobiographies of Elon Musk, Warren Buffett, Steve Jobs, Bill Gates and their ilk, hoping to emulate their trajectory to wealth and status. I wondered if the young reader was totally disinterested and plain embarrassed for me. It was discomforting, toying around with these thoughts.

Amy Spies, the professional writer and writing teacher, however, responded with a suggestion to do a Skype session since she was in the United States. She needed to understand how she could be of help. I spoke to her, a stranger, as if I had known her for years. I saw a mirror reflection of myself in her. We wore our hair in a similar style. She meditated regularly, as I did. She was also a teacher of writing. She had two young adult children. She valued family relationships. She empathized. She showed interest in my dad's story, and in mine. She asked questions. She expressed without hesitation what she found interesting and what she wanted to know more of. She also recommended a few sessions of Mindfulness Writing, which I found profoundly helpful. It helped me to excavate some of the forgotten moments with my dad, moments that were deeply buried in my psyche. I was surprised to discover that most of the forgotten moments were happy ones. Through each Mindfulness writing session, I discovered more and more that I was wallowing in negative thoughts, and there was so much more to celebrate and be grateful for. The moments and personal insights kept emerging after a series of Mindful Writing meditations that Amy offered. I would begin each session with a thought, but by the end of it I would've questioned my position and my assumptions. It was revelatory. I recognized then the value of a writing teacher. She was a critical friend, an agent of provocation and a facilitator of growth. She helped me grow as a writer by suppressing my inner critic and creating space enough for me to continue discovering what I wanted to express.

One of her Mindfulness Writing sessions, for instance, began with an exploration of intentions. My initial response was: I want this memoir of my dad published. That is what matters most at this point in time. But as soon as I wrote those thoughts down, I began to doubt my intentions. Am I doing this, I wondered, for myself? Or was it for my dad? It left me feeling uncomfortable about my true intentions. At the end of the meditation, however, I discovered what I truly wanted out of life now. In the guided meditation, as I submerged myself in the water, instead of enjoying its calm and stillness, instead of floating on my back, eyes closed, I wanted to play; I wanted to splash the shimmering water and enjoy watching the birds flap their wings and take flight. What a beautiful sight it was to watch the birds soar into infinite space. I didn't care anymore about what mattered most or what my intentions were. I felt relaxed. I felt a sudden surge of life force running through my veins, throbbing—my heart felt alive and I began dancing to the tune of the rush. I wanted to be able to play: play with colours, play with words, play with ideas. What I chose to write, and what I chose to paint, took me closer to what I truly am and what I intend to be: I want to be able to play in the garden of life in my twilight years. It may not make sense, but that's what I discovered.

The most beautiful and gratifying part of my journey took me to my children and nephews. I reached out to them and got them to do some writing, using some simple strategies to get them to go way back in time to recall moments past. Recalling past experiences is not as easy as it appears to be. They needed to be gently cajoled out of the intricate folds of the mind. They took some time to get back to me with their written responses, but the outcome was beyond what I had ever imagined.

Chapter 19
DEAR MUTHACHA

THE YEAR IS 2018. It's been fourteen years since my dad left us. My nephew, my dad's first grandchild, Nishanker, is thirty. He is married and lives in Chicago. He did his MBA at the Chicago Booth School of Business, and works at one of the biggest hedge funds in the world as a research analyst. My daughter, Sandhya, dad's second grandchild, is thirty. She is married and lives in Tokyo. She pursued her master's degree at EM Lyon Business School in France. She is a social media manager in her own company. My son is twenty-seven. He graduated from University College London with a Master of Laws in Banking, Corporate, Finance and Security Law. He is still single and eligible. He lives at home currently, and is doing his legal training at my brother's law firm. And then there is the youngest of his grandchildren, my second nephew who, at fourteen, never knew his granddad. He was born in the same year my dad passed on, six months later. He lives in Singapore. I needed to understand what they knew and understood about their granddad. And what it was like for the older three, growing up with their *muthacha* or granddad? What did they remember? What did they not remember? What did they want to remember of their granddad? So, I reached out to them with this question: What would you want your granddad to know if he were listening to you now? The eldest of his grandchildren, my nephew, Nish, wrote:

> *I wish my memories of Muthacha were clearer and easier to recall, but the years have blurred the details somewhat.*

What the years haven't blurred was the quiet and comforting sense of companionship he brought to my childhood. There was always a bit of a language barrier between us, yet in a surprising way, I suspect it simplified our relationship for the better. With Muthacha, there was never pressure to make conversation, or the constant fear of being disciplined that usually arose around other adults. He was content to just hang out with us kids and watch us play, and we were happy to just be kids, doing silly kid things. And when we looked up from our toys and games, there he was—a strong, silent, and contented presence, usually smiling at us, or generally looking bemused by our childish antics. And then we'd go back to playing, comforted to know that we were still under the watchful gaze of someone who cared about us, but not feeling the pressure of having to do anything but be kids. It was truly a remarkable thing. He rarely said much to me, but there was never any doubt in my mind that he loved me. Loved all of us kids. It was obvious in the way he wanted to spend time with us, obvious in the way he would smile at us, occasionally ruffle our hair, occasionally chuckle at something we were doing. Looking back, it's like remembering a master class in non-verbal communication.

I'll never forget the first summer I came back to Singapore after his passing. I walked into the back room in the old house, almost expecting to see him, but he wasn't there. The room looked the same, but he wasn't there. And that's when it really hit me that he was gone. It made me realize how much I had enjoyed having him around, how much it set my mind at ease just knowing he was nearby. I remember crying in that room, but after a few minutes, I also remember feeling like he was there with me. It was such a distinct sensation that it still gives me some comfort to this day, that maybe we'll see each other again. Now that I'm thinking about it, it was that same old sensation that always came with being around Muthacha. I felt safe, I felt comforted, and I felt at ease.

Today, looking back with a 30-year-old's perspective, I wish I could have known him better and I wish we could have had more time together. That said, I also feel like I know what I really needed to know about him. He was a good man who loved his family and grandchildren, and even all these years can't erase the pleasant memory of just being a kid in the presence of a loving grandfather. I'll always be thankful to him for that.

My daughter, his second grandchild wrote:

Dear Muthacha,
    More than anything, I remember your warmth, your smile and that comforting sense of security I felt in your presence.
    After you had your first stroke, on my fifteenth birthday, I was suddenly faced with something I never wanted to think about. In my eyes you were so strong and independent. It broke my heart to see you in a hospital bed, even though you were still smiling and trying to make light of the situation. You did not want us to worry about you, you knew we were scared, and you wanted to comfort us despite your own fears. That sums up who you were as a person.
    You never recovered fully from the damage the stroke did, and things slowly deteriorated from there. I felt like you were easing us into life without you.
    I never remember you angry at me or unhappy at home. You made little jokes or funny noises to make us laugh when we were grumpy or just having a bad day. You tried your best to communicate and bond with us through these small gestures. I still worry we took your positivity and love for granted.
    After we went to bed, you used to, very softly, open our

bedroom door just to check we were in bed. You would gently close the door behind you when you saw we were safely tucked away. You did this not because you were worried we were being naughty and staying up, you did it because you wanted to know we were okay. That we were safe. You could only go to sleep with that in mind.

After you passed away, I kept hearing the spring in the doorknob twist and click, just like it did when you checked up on us. There were so many things about you that I loved dearly and never truly appreciated till you left us.

They might sound like small things, but they created warmth and love in our lives. Your love was genuine and uncomplicated—it was consistent every day, despite the struggles you might have been going through. You were strong for all of us and we were lucky to have experienced love in its purest form.

Sometimes our love for each other is dependent on the mood we're in or what we're going through in life. Not with you. Even though very few words were exchanged between us, I knew you cared and I hope very much that you felt our love, too.

My son, his third grandchild wrote:

My grandfather was someone of very few words. The fact that he spoke little English and I did not speak Malayalam meant verbal communication between us was even more limited. However, this didn't stop him from being close to his grandchildren or stop us from being close to him. Everyone always knew he was around and appreciated as well as constantly felt his presence.

Apart from calling me a "fool," which was thoroughly deserved most of the time, we mainly communicated through eyes and gestures. He would speak in Malayalam. I would speak in English, and ultimately the language of sports brought us together. This is perfectly exemplified in the football games I used to watch with him every weekend. Given our manner of communication, I was extremely lucky to share this with him for ninety minutes every week as we sat down to watch Manchester United. He would always sit in the chair with a brown base and floral-patterned cushions. For those ninety minutes, despite a total lack of verbal communication with each other, everything we would do would be in sync. If a player messed up, we would look to each other with a similar look of displeasure. On the other hand, when we scored (one of the few times he looked expressly overjoyed), we would look at each other and smile. The ninety minutes went by every week with him sitting in the very same chair. Thankfully, the years we watched football together marked the best years of our football club. This meant he and I were often very happy at the end of games and as a kid I enjoyed seeing him like this.

The youngest of my dad's grandchildren is Nikhil. He is fourteen and was born six months after my dad passed on. I sought to understand what he wanted to know about his granddad.

When I visited Nikhil at home, I wasn't quite sure how this teenager was going to respond to my request. Would he think it weird or boring to sit with his aunt and discuss a grandparent that he never knew? I was tentative. When I arrived, he was totally engrossed playing a computer game long-distance with a friend in Kuala Lumpur. Both boys were giving a running commentary on how each was progressing while playing the game. I marveled at their dexterity. They were able to speak to each other and yet swipe their virtual opponents on the giant screen with paint. It was a perfect display of hand-eye coordination. I waited for him to finish his game. Towards the end of one of his games, I had to quickly jump in to express the reason for my visit. I told him I was writing a memoir about his dad's dad, and that it would be dedicated to all four of his grandchildren. And, since he never got to know his granddad, I wanted us to have a chat. He was surprised but very respectful. At the end of that game, he bid his friend adieu, switched off the television and gave me his full attention. My fears were unfounded and I was glad that I had made the effort to reach out to my young nephew.

I asked him if he had any questions about his grandfather. Was there anything he wanted to know? I told him to write down his questions. Nikhil wanted to know what his occupation was and what kind of a father he was, and if he was an "active dad" who went out to play with his children. How much time did he spend with his family? What kind of person was he? How did he treat his family and others? Did he spend most of his time working? I, then, gave Nikhil about fifteen minutes of quiet time to write on one of the questions he had asked about my dad. I was pleasantly surprised to see him fully engaged in penning his thoughts.

Nikhil, the youngest, wrote:

> *As I didn't get to know him at all, I wonder what kind of father he was. He must have been a good one as he raised two very successful children. I want to meet him some day but I can't. I wonder whether he treated his friends and family well. They all seem to miss him very much, and it hurts to know that I've never met him. My father and mother rarely talk about him so I know little to none about him, but every time they do, they always have good things to say. I never really wondered what it would be like if he was here. My father has a tremendous amount of respect for my granddad. Dad would tell me stories like, "Your grandfather was very generous in war times" or "Your grandfather was a good man." So even from my father's words and the amount of respect he had for my grandfather, he must have been a good father.*

The fourteen-year-old had several unanswered questions. He was obviously thinking about fathers and what good fathers were like. Was it just about being a provider? Was there a role fathers could play in being a child's playmate? Could a dad be both a friend and a father? These are the very same questions we grapple with today.

Chapter 20

Dear Acha,

I am moved beyond words by the children's affection for you. I was also pleasantly surprised by their enthusiasm to excavate memories of you, buried and almost lost in time. Reaching out to the children, now young adults, except Nikhil, has triggered fresh memories that I had truly forgotten. I had completely forgotten how much of our social interactions were centred around watching football matches in the living room with you seated in the elephant chair. I remember how Preshin had an ally in you—as you were both crazy German football fans—against Manmindar, Suresh and me, who were diehard Brazilian fans. You would always cheer with gusto for Germany and fume whenever Brazil scored goals during the FIFA World Cup. You knew it infuriated us, but you got a kick out of it simply because you felt, just as Preshin did, that the Brazilian players were all style and no substance, unlike the Germans who were hardworking straight shooters. I remember the FIFA World Cup finals, before I got married, when you were the lone Germany supporter against your two children, Suresh and me. How could I have forgotten those days! It was infectious: the groans, the cheers, the cries, the whistles, the daggers, the smiles, the laughter....

The family trip to Chirayankil completely escaped me as well, until much later. Strangely, seeing you unconscious stimulated an avalanche of feelings that buried all the beautiful experiences that we shared as a family. It was easier to recall the tragic moments, but writing about us has helped me to unearth some of the beautiful experiences we shared together.

I would also like you to know that just the other day, Preshin asked mummy to give him your gold Casio watch, which he wears everywhere he goes now. I think he is basking in your memory, as is Nish, who is waiting to read this memoir. Strangely, or perhaps it's not that strange, that all four of them seem to want to reach out to you and communicate some things to you.

Nish's letter to you was such a gem. He felt the pulse of your love for the family. More importantly, I learnt something from him. For him language was no barrier, and he felt that in fact it simplified the relationship for the better. It's so true: sometimes, or dare I say often, we have a way of placing too much emphasis on words without actually reflecting on how far they are actually capable of reflecting the core of our being. Sometimes we speak for the sake of it. We say things we don't mean. We don't say what we do mean. It's complicated. But with you in the latter years, as Nish says, "There was never pressure to make conversation or be this or that. You just let us be kids, and enjoyed seeing us being naughty, silly or kiddish as kids often are!" How beautiful! How true!

Nikhil, too, surprised me with his questions and his impression of you from the little that we told him. We have taken a lot of things for granted and forgotten the importance of passing on what we know about the people we love, they who have played a vital role in shaping who we have become today.

This morning, dad, is a very special morning. I never expected this day to come so soon. Sandhya is getting married at the Layan Sithi Vinayagar Temple at 9.30. Your granddaughter made me create a spreadsheet with timelines and to-do lists. I need to be in her room by 6 am. She has planned for me to get my hair and make-up done. I couldn't sleep a wink last night. My head kept buzzing with all the things that I had to remember to do to make this occasion *special for Sandhya and Timmy. I had already forgotten one thing from home: the string of jasmine flowers that I had ordered for all the bridesmaids. I am probably as excited as I am anxious to ensure that all goes well at the Hindu Ceremony in the temple. This is the only thing that she put me in charge of, so I better not foul up!*

I set the alarm for 5.00 am to meditate, earlier than I normally do. The room, at the Fullerton Bay Hotel, was dark but I could see Manmindar's silhouette. He was purring gently by my side, oblivious of the butterflies that were fluttering in my stomach. I closed my eyes lightly and sat in a half-lotus position. As soon as the in-breath and out-breath met and blended into each other, I became entranced and still. As always, it felt as if the breath had stopped before the calm begins to quench the soul. An image of you smiling with your dark penetrating eyes emerged before me. I could feel your warmth radiating to fill the room. You looked so happy. Yes, dad! She's getting married in the temple that you used to go to every Friday morning at 6, during the sixteen years you lived with us. It was your weekly pilgrimage. You must be very proud of the reason she chose to get married at this temple. It was small, but for her, it was meaningful because she associated that temple with you. "Muthacha used to go to that temple, right, mum? Then, you and dad on Mondays?" Sandhya was particular. I had chosen a bigger temple earlier that would provide convenient parking for the guests, but she wasn't impressed. She walked into the temple and she walked out. "No, mum!" That's your granddaughter. The cosy Ganesha temple it was!

As I enter the room, I see Sandhya, glowing, with the sun rising behind her in Marina Bay Sands. I know you are here with us. I can feel the warmth of your smile radiating. And I just know that you will be there to ensure everything goes well, and it did.

When Nish got married in Chicago six months ago to Rachel, there was the same warmth radiating in the South Shore Community Hall facing Lake Michigan. I felt your presence. It was a similarly blissful day. There was so much warmth and goodwill. It was a lovely reunion! All of us from Singapore were there, including another new member of the family, Sandhya's fiancé, Timmy!

Mummy was there, too, though she nearly missed Nish's special day. We came very close to losing mummy two years ago, nine months before Nish's wedding. It was a random day and a random fall. It had been a fine sunny afternoon. We were on our way out for lunch when she slipped on the wet floor at home and hit her head. The slow bleed on both sides of her brain impaired her movement and coordination. We noticed that she picked up everything with her left hand though she was right-handed, and her right leg lagged behind her as she walked. We fortunately got her to the emergency unit in time. The moments before and after the surgery were poignant. Mum had our undivided attention. She displayed extraordinary courage. Mum's recovery from the brain surgery was miraculous, and what was even more magical was her will to travel all the way to Chicago for Nish's wedding. During the critical period in hospital awaiting the surgical procedure, she said that she had experienced a near-death experience because her blood pressure dipped to dangerously low levels. She drifted off, but she was brought back by the nurses in attendance. I remember speaking to you then, dad, to please spare her.

Just as the children had enjoyed having you around, they have been fortunate to get to know their grandmother better. They are always teasing mummy about her eating habits, and reminding her to go for her walks. They insist on taking her for all the big events, even if it means taking long haul flights. She attended Preshin's graduation in London and has been coming with us for most of our family holidays, just as you did.

She appears in the grandchildren's Instagram and Facebook pages, and Preshin just called her a "celebrity grandmother." "All my friends love you, Muthi. Do you know how lucky you are? You don't have to say anything and do anything and everybody loves you."

They are not allowing their grandmother to grow old and forgetful. . . and forgotten! And neither am I, dad! You'll always be remembered as a loving, most generous and giving father.

Do you recognize this mountain, dad? It was one of the first memories I chose to paint. There was a mountain, solid and steady in the background as I looked upwards, mesmerised by the Sakura blossoms verdant and pink on brown twiggy branches, standing perfectly symmetrical and majestic. That mountain remained unmoved in the midst of the clarion call for spring to display its beauty. I see how you were always that mountain: strong, silent and majestic, always there, in the distance, watching us with calm confidence.

Chapter 21

Dear Shali,

    I am immensely moved by the children's letters. I enjoy watching them and watching over them, every day. They have grown in ways I imagined they would. They are affectionate children and they have so much love for mummy. I sometimes envy the relationship they have with mummy. They keep pulling her legs—how they know her! Her whims and fancies, her love for sweets and chocolates, rice, noodles and milk. Her love for all things beautiful. Her love for colour and life! I love how mummy still enjoys draping herself in all six yards of colourful silk threads! I laugh every time Preshin keeps reminding her that she is not a baby to be drinking so much milk. It's fattening, muthi, all this milk and sugar you have with your coffee! But she brushes it off. "Milk is good for you. Brown sugar and especially gula Melaka is good for you." It is full of minerals and nutrients, just like the molasses she would happily add to her coffee. But Preshin carries on, just as unfazed as his grandmother, in reminding her to take her walks and eat right. I am so thankful!

    I am pleasantly surprised at how assertive mummy has become. She seems to have an opinion on everything, and she seems to be expressing it with such confidence. She is even critiquing your art pieces with such authority. I see how you are being surrounded by well-meaning critics at home. You mustn't take them too seriously. You will find your way through the mountain, and turn the arduous hike into a walk in the park. Keep writing. Keep painting. Keep scaling that mountain!

And with regard to Malayalam and the fatherland, India will always have a special place in my heart. It's where our roots lie: strong and deep. Its rich history and culture will no doubt add to our understanding of who we are, but Singapore gave us the opportunities to spread our branches and flower, drawing from the deep wealth of a civilization that has existed for thousands of years. I never worried about how Malayalam got spoken less and less at home. It didn't matter. What mattered was you wanting to reach out and touch souls regardless of race, language or religion. Sometimes, all you need is to light your path with love to connect deeply. In my new existence, I have found a spaciousness and expansiveness. There are no oceans, seas or mountains separating us. Where I am, space and time collapses into oblivion. There is no tomorrow, no yesterday. We are here and now. We are one. We are from the same source of light and return to that source we will, regardless of who we are, and where we are from, after we fulfill our life's purpose. So, no regrets, no judgments, and forgive we must as we journey towards the source.

Until we meet in the light,
Hugs and kisses to all,
Acha

My nephew, Nishanker's wedding celebrations at South Shore Community Hall, Chicago, August 2017.
Standing from left: Timmy (then Sandhya's fiancé), Sandhya (my daughter), Manmindar (my husband), Shalini, Indira (my mum), Rachael (the bride), Nishanker (the groom), Suresh (my brother) and Preshin (my son)

Sandhya's wedding eclebrations in Singapore, April 2018.
Standing from left: Manmindar, Shalini, Timmy (the groom), Sandhya (the bride), grandma Indira and Preshin

Four grandchildren to whom *Dad and I* is dedicated to with their grandma at Fullerton Bay Hotel Singapore, April 2018.
Standing from left: Preshin, Nishanker, Nikhil and Sandhya with grandma Indira or Muthi

The Mountain Rises

*The mountain rises
Silent and Still,
Fearless and Free.
It stands tall, for you and me.*

*If invisible and impervious still,
Those shrouds of wispy clouds
You may whoosh away
With deep ocean breaths.*

*Beckon, invite, drop in,
Or fixing your gaze,
Meditate, muse or ruminate
Till you rekindle and reconnect.*

ACKNOWLEDGMENTS

I WOULD LIKE TO thank my patient and loving mum, without whom this memoir would not have been possible. She would tell and retell some of the stories about my dad until I got it. And thanks to my husband, Manmindar, for his unconditional love and faith in me. He was the first to give me his response to my first ten chapters. Manmindar, thank you for your encouragement in helping me to grow, and develop the potential you saw in me. To my brother, Suresh, for allowing me to piggyback on his exciting life and retell some of his stories. I am also grateful to Marion Neubronner, my friend and informal coach, for literally kickstarting this endeavor with her openness and sincerity. Also Amy Spies, my writing teacher, for helping me conquer my inner critic; for providing me with her "first blush impressions," and for her heartfelt rejoinders that gave me insights into how readers from a different world would respond to the cultural and historical contexts in which some of the stories unfolded. After several sessions with Amy, I realized that we are more alike than unlike, in spite of the oceans that separate people who hail from different countries and eras. I also benefited a great deal from her "Mindful Writing" sessions that helped me to dive into myself and deepen my writing. Thank you for all your words of encouragement, and for making me believe in the writer in myself. I would also like to express my heartfelt gratitude to Dr. Anitha Devi Pillai, my friend, lecturer and teacher educator at the National Institute of Education, for having so kindly agreed to read my final manuscript. I was overwhelmed by her spontaneous response, thoughtful criticisms and edits. Thank you for believing in me and encouraging me to publish my memoir. I am also immensely grateful to Guy Vincent, Tre Wee and Wendolin Perla of Publishizer for their outstanding support, through whom this publishing deal with Koehler Books was made possible. And to John Koehler of Koehler Books my deepest appreciation for believing in this book, and for his patience in guiding me through the publishing process, as a first time author. To his team: Joe Coccaro, Executive Editor, Elizebeth Marshall McClure, copy editor and Skyler Kratofil, illustrator and designer, my heartfelt thanks for their professionalism and warm support. Last but not least, my children, Sandhya and Preshin, and my nephews, Nishanker and Nikhil, for cheering me on to the finish line with their letters to my dad. Their expressions of love moved me to tears.

To all of you beautiful people, my heartfelt appreciation. I feel very blessed to have you in my life.

Special Thanks

AS A FIRST-TIME AUTHOR, the experience of writing *Dad and I* posed several challenges, but reaching out to friends to pre-order my book while it was still at the manuscript stage was even more daunting. I wasn't quite sure how my family and friends, and former students and colleagues would respond. The fear of rejection was real! I was, however, pleasantly surprised by the number of people who rose to the occasion in a gesture of goodwill to give me the encouragement and support I needed. The interest many expressed in my book was heart-warming and rewarding in itself. I want to take this opportunity to thank each and every subscriber who helped make my campaign to pre-sell *Dad and I* successful. We pre-sold 500 books, thanks to you. I wish I could name each and every one of you here, but rest assured I will always be indebted to you, and I want you to know that you have made the world a better place by giving an unknown writer like me a chance to find an excellent publisher.

My special thanks also to:

My corporate sponsors who pre-ordered more than 25 copies of *Dad and I*, Ms Antoinette Biehlmeier, founder of TheraSmart and owner of InnerDynamics Map; and Mr. Suresh Damodara, managing director of Damodara Ong LLC

My subscribers who pre-ordered more than 10 copies of *Dad and I*, Desmond Chia, Fiona Lee, Nikhil Ming Damodara, Sukhmohinder

Singh, Vincent Lee, Margaret Tan, Sandhya and Timmy Chie, and Padmini Panicker

My subscribers with 5 pre-orders of *Dad and I*, Alan Cheok, Yeo Boon Hong, Chandri Gunawardhana, Jennifer Lui, Lynette Ng, Lisa Tan, Rita Danani, Rita Fernandez, Sanjay Kuttan, Sunu Sivadasan, S. Chandrasegaran and Shanavas Vijayan.

As promised, I look forward to running some of my Mindfulness programmes for you. Please log onto lovingmybreath.com to register your interest and preference.

Lightning Source UK Ltd.
Milton Keynes UK
UKHW040853160120
357069UK00001B/156/P